Black Wave

BLACK WAVE

A FAMILY'S ADVENTURE *at* SEA
and the DISASTER *That* SAVED THEM

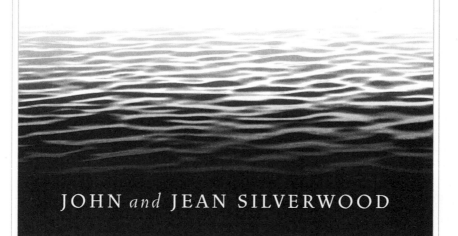

JOHN *and* JEAN SILVERWOOD

RANDOM HOUSE NEW YORK

Published in the United States by Random House, an imprint of
The Random House Publishing Group, a division of Random House, Inc.,
New York.

RANDOM HOUSE and colophon are registered trademarks
of Random House, Inc.

Except where noted, all photographs courtesy of the Silverwood family.

LIBRARY OF CONGRESS CATALOGING-IN-PUBLICATION DATA

Silverwood, John.
Black wave: a family's adventure at sea and the disaster that saved them / John and
Jean Silverwood.
p.   cm.
ISBN 978-1-4000-6655-1
1. Silverwood, John—Travel.   2. Silverwood, Jean—Travel.   3. Silverwood,
John—Family.   4. *Emerald Jane* (Catamaran)   5. Ocean travel.   6. Yachting.
7. Yachting injuries.   8. Yachting accidents.   9. Manuae (French Polynesia)—
Description and travel.   10. Adventure and adventurers—United States—
Biography.   I. Silverwood, Jean.   II. Title.
G530.S5755 2008   910.9164'—dc22   2007036610

Printed in the United States of America on acid-free paper

www.atrandom.com

2 4 6 8 9 7 5 3 1

First Edition

Book design by Liz Cosgrove

With love and gratitude,
to our parents, Albert, Jane, John, and Patricia,
and four children, Ben, Amelia, Jack, and Camille

A great rolling sea, dashing high up against the reeling ship's high teter-ing side, stove in the boat's bottom at the stern, and left it again, all drip-ping through like a sieve.

"Bad work, bad work! Mr. Starbuck," said Stubb, regarding the wreck, "but the sea will have its way. Stubb, for one, can't fight it. You see, Mr. Starbuck, a wave has such a great long start before it leaps, all round the world it runs, and then comes the spring! But as for me, all the start I have to meet it, is just across the deck here."

—*Herman Melville,* MOBY DICK

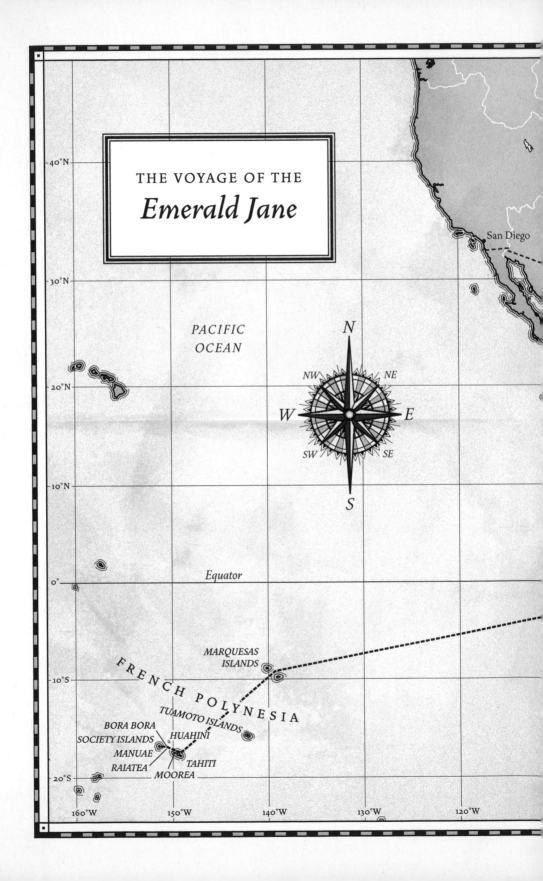

THE VOYAGE OF THE
Emerald Jane

PACIFIC
OCEAN

N

NW   *NE*

W   *E*

SW   *SE*

S

San Diego

Equator

MARQUESAS
ISLANDS

F R E N C H   P O L Y N E S I A

TUAMOTO ISLANDS

BORA BORA
SOCIETY ISLANDS   *HUAHINI*
MANUAE
RAIATEA   *TAHITI*
MOOREA

40°N

30°N

20°N

10°N

0°

10°S

20°S

160°W   150°W   140°W   130°W   120°W

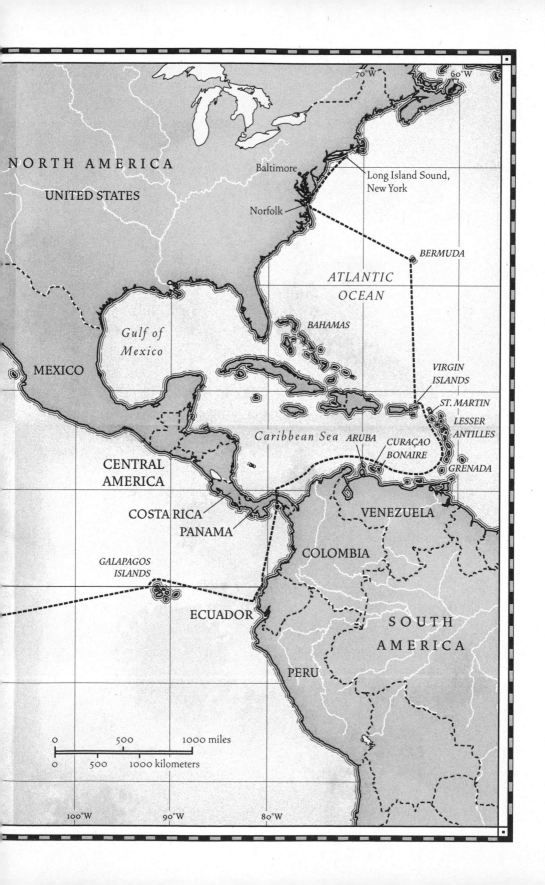

CONTENTS

BOOK I

BOOK II

——

BOOK I

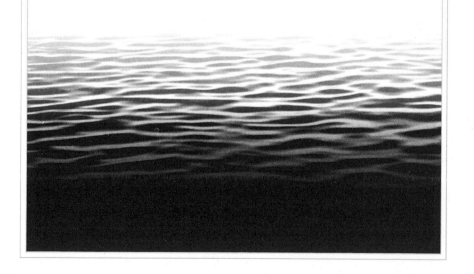

[1]

A HEART-SHAPED REEF

In the same hour that the Emerald Jane *was approaching Scilly Island in the South Pacific, my sister-in-law was alone in her New York home. A sharp crash made her jump: A watercolor of a racing sailboat had fallen from her wall to the hardwood floor. A wedding present from John and me, it had hung in the same spot for twenty-one years. Joanne, a little shaken, started calling around the family to find where we might be—she knew we were somewhere far at sea.*

———

Below deck in our catamaran sailboat, my husband, John, stood in the doorway of our tiny stateroom. I can picture him there in that instant before everything changed. Our four children—we had pried them away from their suburban world for a thousand reasons—were busy elsewhere on the boat, settling in for the night. John had just told me how long it would probably take us to get to Fiji, our next destination by way of Tonga; some problems with the boom of the mainsail were slowing us down, but we could fix it in the morning. After Fiji, we would head for Australia. From there, the kids and I were planning to head home to the States, and John would stay long enough to clean up *Emerald Jane* and sell her—which can take months, and I worried about that. I guess I was worried about what might become of our marriage after this long adventure. I was also worried about the whole idea of selling a ship that had become like one of the family; I thought it would be particularly hard on John, who loved her the most.

We had done what we set out to do two years earlier when we first set sail. Along the way, our children's eyes had opened to the beauty of the world. The kids were very strong characters now, very different from when we began. We loved them in new ways—maybe deeper ways, because we had taken the time to finally get to know them.

John said he had just finished a sweet conversation under the stars with Amelia, our fourteen-year-old daughter, during her turn at the wheel. She had followed him back inside and, by tossing the life vest to her sixteen-year-old brother, Ben, turned the "watch" over to him. He had been watching the movie *Drop Dead Gorgeous* on a laptop. Movies on DVD were a vestige of our once and future life, and Ben needed a dose of that now and then, as did we all. The boat was on automatic pilot as Ben prepared to go aft for his two-hour watch.

Everybody was finally happy to be together—it had taken a few thousand miles, but the family now seemed in synch and content. I don't mean that it was perfect, but we had learned to live together in a tight space without too much drama.

We had about a minute left.

With our autopilot engaged, the boat was sailing itself in this moment. We thought.

I was propped up in bed with a laptop as John chatted from the doorway. He looked good. He is a handsome, green-eyed guy full of fun and energy. People sometimes say he looks like Dennis Quaid. Maybe so.

He does have strong features and he's certainly handsome. He has serious eyes that always give away what he's thinking. He has, or rather had, a dark mustache. Amelia and I talked him into throwing it overboard during the long sail across the Pacific. He's even better-looking without it.

He hadn't had a drink since his big meltdown in the Caribbean, and I was pretty much in love with him again.

So you can picture the crew: Amelia looks a little older than her fourteen years. She has long, dark strawberry blond hair, and big, empathetic brown eyes. She is very fit, with a great, honest smile and the hint of dimples. She is very pretty and has a natural charisma that has always filled the space around her. She is eminently sensible, a peacemaker, Daddy's girl. Ben, her older brother by a year and a half, is the surfer archetype: very blond hair, dazzling blue eyes, great smile when it breaks through the gloom of family unfairness, tallish to the point where he sometimes stoops a bit to fit into a crowd. Despite his rock shirts and his surfer looks, you would say he appears quite respectable: a top achiever in Scouts, perhaps, which is exactly right. Little green-eyed Camille, five, has long golden hair, pink cheeks, and a huge smile, which is nearly always beaming. Jack, her freckled nine-year-old brother, seems to have stepped out of an old Our Gang film: the neighborhood tough guy. His mouth is always a little open in wonder. His blond hair and hazel eyes are usually seen only in the blur of his constant explorations. My own hair is long and blond and my eyes are brown, like Amelia's. I do apologize for the fact that we might seem like Southern California stereotypes. Guilty, I suppose.

It was just after dark in a lonely reach of the South Pacific. As we sped westward, the ocean floor was a mile below us—or it was supposed to be.

Then at that moment everything changed.

Like when microphone feedback suddenly fills an auditorium until you must cover your ears, a deafening shrill exploded through the boat. It seemed to come from everywhere. A big jostle. Horrible, gouging, scraping chalkboardlike sounds. The twin hulls under us were screaming. John looked at me the way someone in the next seat of an airplane might look if, at forty thousand feet, all the engines just quit. I had never seen him so instantly confused and horrified—then came the great shaking and crash as we bounced more violently between the iron-hard treetops of submerged coral, sharp as butcher knives. Seconds later we slammed full-on into the coral reef. Our home, the *Emerald Jane,* came to a ripping halt, and the great waves of the Pacific exploded around us in a deafening, continuous roar. John caught himself against the doorway. "My God!" he shouted, his eyes drilling crazily into mine. Everything about our lives had just changed and we knew it. Our lives, our children's lives, could end in the dark of the sea in what? A minute from now? Less?

"Reef!" Ben screamed from the deck.

"It can*not* be coral! We're miles . . ." John yelled to himself and me as he bounded up the small stairway—I was right behind him.

"Dad! Dad! What's happening?" Amelia shouted over the roaring surf and the loud tearing of the boat against the coral. She tried to cut him off in the salon. The *Drop Dead* laptop was dead on the floor; things had fallen everywhere. Our two younger kids, Jack and Camille, were on the salon's big wraparound sofa under the front windows, petrified and gritting their teeth, their eyes incredibly wide and their hands hovering in front of them with their little fingers outstretched, shaking.

"It's a reef, guys. We're on a reef. We'll be fine," John said without stopping, pushing Amelia aside and running aft through the open glass door of the salon and leaping up the step to the teak deck of the cockpit. His eyes were terrified and the kids saw that. They had never seen him like this before—though they had seen a lot. Then I came through behind him, grabbed flashlights, and they saw my eyes. I didn't believe John's quick analysis that we'd be fine. The kids took no comfort in it either. His eyes, truer than his lips, were saying, *we are in very serious trouble.*

He had been so careful to navigate us far around the coral atoll islands in this stretch of sea. Back in Tahiti, he had replaced the autopilot's computer to make sure we had the very best.

As we looked over the edge of the deck into the dark sea—the moon had not yet risen—our flashlights revealed millions of hard, red fingers of coral tearing at our boat through the boiling surf. Our lights would not last for long, and John would soon be asking Ben to take a knife and do the unthinkable. So much would happen this night in the dark.

John threw the engine hard into reverse just as a high wave crested violently over the stern and over him with a loud crash. The double hulls smashed again with a horrible sound into the coral. He leapt through the flash flood on deck to reach the controls of the other engine. He hit the start button and pushed it hard into reverse. Both engines could not even begin to pull the boat off the reef.

Only the front, smaller jib sail, called the genoa and nicknamed the genny, had been in use. It absolutely had to be hauled down this instant if the engines were to have any chance. John pulled the genny's thick Dacron line off one of the two stainless-steel, hourglass-shaped winches behind the wheels. The wind should have instantly spilled from the sail, but, in the windy whip and tangle of the moment, the line had jammed in a pulley somewhere forward. Ben, enough of a sailor now to understand that the sail had to be cut, snapped the handle of a diving knife into his father's hand.

John zigzagged forward along the lurching deck. Crouching near the bow, he cut the line. As the genny snapped free to flap in the wind, the large metal reinforced tip of the sail—where the lines tie on—whistled toward his face. He leapt backward as it just missed his eyes; he had seen the glint of it coming thanks to flashlights Ben and Amelia were now shining forward from the aft deck.

The surf roared like a tumble of jet engines all around us. We were screaming to each other just to be heard.

I ran into the salon to help get the kids ready for our escape. Little Jack and Camille were still frozen in fear on the wraparound sofa—just sitting there hugging each other and shaking horribly. There were loud popping and cracking sounds. Looking down the stairs into the port hull, I was suddenly watching a disaster movie; it couldn't be real: Water was filling the starboard hull as if a dam had burst. The view down the little stairway was of water rushing floor to ceiling from Amelia's room toward Ben's. Her tennis shoes and bedclothes and books were swirling in the flood. Then the retreat of the sea pulled the water back toward Amelia's room, drawing Ben's things into the swirl, then back again. With each surge, the water was lapping higher up the steps toward the salon where we stood frozen, watching, maybe screaming. It couldn't be real. The boat was being devoured now with each great wave.

Amelia and I grabbed canvas shopping totes and started collecting some of the flotsam that might be useful in the life raft, especially bottles of water and packages of food. Our hands were shaking so violently that it was hard to pick things up and put them in the bags—and I was slipping terribly on the wood floor. Jack said something but I could not make it out. "What, Jack?" I screamed over the din of crashing surf and cracking boat.

"I don't want to die," he screamed back.

"Me either!" little Camille screamed.

"We don't want to die!" they screamed together.

Amelia was handling this better then I was; she put her arms around both of them.

"Don't worry," she said, "we have two other boats, remember? This is what they are for—just this kind of thing. It happens all the time." They calmed down and sat back to watch this disaster movie. But they were shaking like we were.

I stepped outside to see how John and Ben were doing. They would have to get the emergency life raft going somehow. The other boat, the dinghy, wouldn't last long swinging there on the stern in this surf.

The coral's digestion of the boat had now become a steady fusillade of earsplitting cracks and pops as the hulls and bulkheads—remarkably strong carbon-fiber laminates—cracked apart. Our belongings began to wash around us. Even above this sound, a new, deep roar behind the boat made all the flashlight beams shine aft to reveal a cresting wave building high above us. Down it came, ripping the dinghy and its stainless-steel davits from the deck. The stern of *Emerald Jane* rose up and crashed on top of the loosened dinghy.

Even without the genny pulling the boat farther into the coral, our engines were useless against the power of the waves and the tightening grip of the coral.

"The radio!" John screamed as he passed by me in the cockpit. He headed through the open glass doors into the salon, where he stood for a second in shock to see the interior awash. He turned to Ben and pointed to the GPS position readout at the chart table. Somewhere in that instant, Ben found a pencil and scrap of paper to write down our position. John and I went the few steps down into the port hull, sloshing but not too deep yet, where the SSB radio was still getting power. John dialed in the emergency frequency and put the microphone close to his mouth to be heard over the roar of our destruction. We were standing in water and operating electrical equipment; I prayed that everything was grounded properly.

"Mayday! Mayday! Mayday! This is sailing vessel *Emerald Jane*. We have struck a reef in position"—Ben reached down the stairs to hand him the scrap of paper—"approximately 16 degrees, 35 minutes south . . . We are sinking and in need of immediate assistance. Mayday. Mayday . . ."

Ben, seeing the fear in the eyes of the little ones, joined Amelia in offering some comfort. He scooped his little brother up and held him close as he turned on the less useful VHF radio in the salon and tried for an acknowledgment from a passing airliner or another ship. Nothing. Our lights began to flicker.

[2]

THE DARK

John was never afraid of the dark—it had always been his friend. He was most himself, in fact, when far out in space, sailing through the stars, leaning into the great curve of the Milky Way. If you have ever been miles from shore in a small craft on a moonless night, with fathomless water all around you reflecting the stars above, you know what it is like to stand at the wheel and navigate your free fall through the universe. If you are sailing with John, he will remind you that Earth and its companions are traveling through the Milky Way at a certain speed—John knows what it is—and he will tell you that the galaxy itself is traveling at a still greater speed through the diamond field of other galaxies, like glittering gowns spinning around endlessly.

He will remind you, as you make your way through the night sea, that you are, in fact, steering a course through the stars. Our galaxy makes the big turns, of course, but you can make some zigs and zags for yourself. And out there on a good sailing night, with the sea gently slapping the bottom of the boat and the ocean air forever freshening your skin and your senses, you experience a perfection of awareness with each bounce of the sea and every breath of breeze.

John always took the late-night watch as the children and I slept below. He sailed us through the universe, as I'd thought he might when I married him nearly twenty years earlier. Many nights on this long journey he would wake up our little sweet-tooth Jack with the aroma of fresh-broken chocolate—we had bought a chest full of five-pound ingots in Panama—so he would have a few nightly hours in space with his father. Then he would send Jack back to bed and he would be alone again up there, taking us through the night into the beauty and genius of the real world, unfiltered even by a Cousteau, watching his compass but, like Peter Pan, also his stars—as in, *second to the right and straight on 'til morning.*

There is a hidden reef ahead somewhere—but isn't there always? We are mortals resigned to that ending. When it arrives so unexpectedly in the night, ready to take not only you but your children, you will pray aloud for the morning. But it happens. It has happened so many times. So many ships have gone down in the coral, and children have slipped into the dark sea. It had happened before on this very reef, long ago. We were replaying history in an awful way.

———

In the flickering lights of the salon, I struggled with our third radio: the handheld satellite phone. I turned it on though my hands were shaking so hard that I dropped it. I held it again in the uncontrolled claws my hands had become. "No signal," the display read. I dropped it again—and now in the water. After that, even the "no signal" display was gone.

"Mayday! Mayday! Mayday!" John repeated into the main radio's microphone. French voices were having a conversation on the frequency. He didn't know if they could hear him; he couldn't get their attention.

The boat heaved higher onto the reef, slamming down and grinding sideways into the coral. The water in Amelia and Ben's hull continued sloshing wildly back and forth, moving ever higher into the salon as the hulls were digested.

Water was now flooding the port hull where John was on the radio. Jack's plastic action heroes, Camille's stuffed animals and Lego toys, washed around him as he shouted for an acknowledgment.

"Pardon! Pardon! Mayday!" But they continued chatting.

We were now all being thrown violently about—the kids riding the sofa with their arms desperately around each other.

John changed frequencies: "Mayday. Mayday. Mayday," he called again. "This is sailing vessel *Emerald Jane.* We have struck a reef … We are sinking and in need of immediate assistance. Mayday. Mayday …" No response. He changed frequencies again.

We had been sailing with only our smaller front sail, plus one of our two engines, because the pin connecting the heavy boom of the mainsail to the mast had come loose in some difficult winds. It proved too difficult to fix in the dark. Had the boat's lopsided thrust somehow defeated our autopilot and sent us the wrong way? Was the new electronic compass faulty? Was the ocean current stronger than we estimated when we were adrift, trying to fix the boom? Was the scale of our map too large for accurate navigation—or was the map just wrong? I couldn't get my mind around it. We had seen the palm trees of this tiny island—or what we thought was this island—hours ago as we dined at sunset.

For whatever reason, this little world of ours was now in fatal peril. It was being pulled by wind and pushed by sea ever farther into the teeth of the reef.

A coral reef is a living thing, millions of years old, but living. It comes up from the bottom with sheer, mile-high underwater cliffs. At the surface, it makes an island or a ring of razor-sharp coral, or both. Sometimes its long ridges lurk just below the surface of the water, where boats will be snagged and quicky destroyed in the surf.

Nothing makes you study your charts more then the idea of hitting a coral reef, with its ragged edges so sharp and diamond-hard they will cut your skin at the touch. They will slice open boat hulls of the thickest steel. I still couldn't believe we had hit one. I couldn't believe what I was seeing with my own eyes, that something beyond my worst nightmare was actually happening. It was. It was happening in this moment. This was somehow real. I could barely grasp that. Not a DVD. Not a DVD.

[3]

THE MAST

I braced myself against the salon's chart table and listened to John's frantic Maydays below. I tried to have one clear thought. Just one. I had considered every emergency but not really this. My mind had nowhere to go with what I was seeing: a boat sinking and my family about to die. I dashed down near John and pulled our emergency radio beacon from the cabinet. Bright yellow, it is about the size and shape of a jumbo soft drink from a convenience market, with a clear dome lid and an antenna coming out the top like a drinking straw. It floats, has a strobe light inside its clear dome, and is supposed to send your GPS location and your boat's I.D. to a satellite monitored by the Coast Guard. I pushed it into John's hands. He stared at it for a long second, wondering if this moment was real. Yes. He turned it on—for whatever it might be worth. Maybe it would help someone find our bodies in a few days—maybe only that. "Hold it upright," he yelled to me as he handed it back. I had something to do.

Big structural bulkheads were cracking and splintering wildly now as if blasted by artillery. The *Emerald Jane* was coming apart rapidly and with dangerous explosions of wood, plastic, and metal.

John gave up on the radio. He bounded up the stairs and looked at Ben. "Life raft!" he shouted over the sounds, and the two of them were gone.

"Come on," I told the three kids in the salon, "let's gather as much food as we can find."

We jammed more bottled water, the handheld VHF radio, a plastic flare box, and canned food into the canvas shopping bags as the water in the salon rose in waves. I smelled the sharp ozone of electrical wires shorting out. The lights flickered and dimmed. Then they went out.

On deck, John and Ben made their way forward with flashlights along the bucking starboard hull. Their objective was to free the inflatable life raft from its deep locker in the deck next to the mast. As high waves swept over them, they stopped every few feet to hold on.

John lowered himself into the locker on his back. He pushed the heavy fiberglass unit upward to Ben, who knelt and pulled as the boat bucked violently. It took two attempts to get the heavy raft out of the slippery pit. They pulled the inflation handle and heard the solid roar of compressed gas as the raft's big doughnut filled and a red canopy roof popped up like a camping tent. They struggled with it in the surf, then lashed it to the netting between the twin bows. As there was no stretch of water that was not packed with sharp coral or crashing surf, there was simply nowhere to go with the raft for now.

Water in the dark salon was knee-high when they returned. Amelia had managed to quiet the kids. She was now holding the rescue radio beacon; its red glow illuminated her face in the dark boat.

"Dad, will we have to walk on the coral?" she asked. He looked down at all our bare feet and quickly found our big basket of beach sandals. "Get 'em on," he ordered.

We suddenly felt the stern rising impossibly high, as before a great fall. The fall came with an earsplitting noise as the *Emerald Jane*'s carbon-fiber spine broke like a twig in a tornado.

We all looked at each other and knew without saying that we needed to be ready to go now, coral or not. If we were going to die, we were going to die with our flip-flops on. We were going to be *doing* something, not standing waiting for death.

While Amelia and I hauled the emergency supplies out onto the aft deck, John and Ben leapt back on deck and, between waves, crawled forward to get the raft and somehow bring it closer to the cockpit, where it could more easily be launched into the sea and where it would be closer to the supplies and to all of us. Amelia brought the little kids out on the stern and we waited to abandon ship. I pulled water bottles from the little refrigerator in the cockpit and handed them, with a flashlight, the emergency beacon, Speedy the turtle, and a prayer stone I somehow had in my hand, to Amelia. I told her to guard the beacon well—it would save us if anything could. She clutched it tightly as the surf sprayed over us and we hung on to the rocking deck.

Another great wave lifted the stern of the boat. The broken spine now allowed the whole length of the *Emerald Jane* to flex like an old shoe. This flex loosened the front line between the bow and the top of the eight-story mast, which in turn allowed the lines supporting the mast from the aft to pull the entire mast backward, out of its base fitting on the deck. The entire 2,500-pound metal mast was now sideways in the air like a baton. The huge mast, the great pride of the *Emerald Jane* and the symbol of the ship's power, crashed down sideways across the bow, just fore of the salon. It grazed Ben's head, gouging him with a metal flange that sent blood streaming down his face. The mast also knocked John backward. He hit his head on the deck so hard he didn't know for a few seconds that the mast was lying across his left leg, just below his knee. He didn't know that one of the winglike line-spreaders attached halfway up the mast had come down like a cleaver and cut through all of his left leg, about seven inches below his knee—cut through all but a few shreds of skin and tendon.

The sea was so violent and the ship so loud with its own destruction that the huge mast crashing down was just another noise in the dark to Amelia, the little kids, and me, waiting on the stern for the life raft. What we heard after the crash of the mast—a very different sound rising over the roar—was John's horrible scream.

John's brain was sorting out the pain from both his head and his leg. An electric pain shot up from his leg through his body and mind. A wave broke over the deck and submerged him. The water was at first a comfort, but then the panic of not being able to struggle to the surface took hold. He felt sheer panic until the wave subsided, and then he screamed for air. He watched his body begin to twist involuntarily on the deck—a tortured man. His eyes rolled back to their whites. He recognized a ragged voice as his own and knew he had screamed. He closed his mouth as it began to fill from yet another sea wave. The suck of the retreating water tugged hard at his body, dragging his arms back. The pain overwhelmed all his thoughts but one: He remembered our son, who might be dead under the mast.

"Ben! Ben! Are you all right?" he yelled into the roar.

"Yeah, Dad," Ben yelled back as he struggled free of tangled lines and steel cables. The life raft was lying over John. Ben thought his father's scream had been about that. He lifted it off his father. Using a glow stick for light, he saw his dad's leg pinned by the mast and nearly cut off by the spreader. Ben's own face ran with blood and salt water, which now poured over his father as he stooped to examine the horrible wound. On his knees, Ben braced against a savage breaker. He held on, staring into his father's eyes, dripping his blood into his father's, awaiting captain's orders.

"Ben, I'm trapped, buddy. Can you move the mast? I think it broke my leg."

Ben struggled to lift the mast. No way. Ton and a quarter, held in place by inch-thick steel cables. John screamed as another wave shifted the weight. Ben crouched low to get leverage—his arms were now clasped around the slick mast, the veins on his neck straining. The next wave moved things again and Ben lifted harder. He got another glimpse of the nearly severed leg and saw a flood of blood spilling under the mast.

John couldn't see for himself over the mast, but, judging from Ben's eyes, it was bad. He pulled Ben close. The roar of the sea and the breaking boat was still a deafening crash. Ben was shaken, dazed for a moment, nauseous. He had seen his father's shredded leg—nearly cut through and pulsing with black blood from the severed arteries and broken bones, all laid out to see.

"You've got to take over now, son. Make the decisions. I can't do anything from here."

Ben nodded, "It'll be okay, Dad. I'm gonna get you out of here."

Pain then overwhelmed him—white light, brilliant and hot. His mouth and eyes froze open. Time stopped for him.

Incoming waves again and again covered John and slightly lifted the tangle of debris—not enough for him to escape, but enough for the weight of the mast to come down again and again, and for the spreader to cut back and forth into his remaining flesh.

Alone under the mast, John knew he had to escape somehow. He propped himself upright and bent forward to grab the mast—a nearly impossible feat had he not been in such good shape. His grip slipped with the next wave and he fell back again. Pain overwhelmed him once more, and the sea covered him again. He was now wild with the mad energy of a trapped animal. He rose from the water and again lurched forward to grab the mast, his adrenaline in full flood. Hanging on to the mast, he could see over it to the white of his shattered bones. He screamed, "Ben, get me some three-eighths-inch line from the cockpit locker—I need to make a tourniquet here fast." A wave knocked him flat and he went mad with the pain.

Ben was back moments later and had to remind John why he brought the line. The pain had pushed rational thought and memory away. John soon remembered. He sat up and reached forward to wrap the line around his leg below the knee, but the spreader was in the way. He had to wrap the line above his left knee, where he twisted it in his fist. Blood was rapidly pooling across the deck, even with the constant rinsing of the waves. A great breaker crashed over John and he lost his grip on the knot. Ben took over, slipping two long screwdrivers under the slack in the line and twisting them in opposite directions to tighten the tourniquet.

I didn't know what had happened—what the scream had meant—until Ben came running for the line.

"Dad is hurt bad," he yelled close to my ear. I turned to Amelia and shouted for her to protect the little ones. She looked at me, and I saw in that instant how she would look as a twenty- or even thirty-year-old. I saw the maturity that had been growing inside her. She nodded.

I followed Ben forward, slipping in the seawater and blood. I stood in shock as Ben worked John's tourniquet. Ben was a mess of blood—his own and his father's. After he tightened the clamp, he leaned close to his father and cried. He was saying goodbye.

"Dad, I'm sorry for the way I've been on the trip. I've treated you and everyone else really horribly. I'm sorry, I'm so sorry."

This moment was suspended in time. The sound of the sea and the crunching, crunching of the boat were still overwhelming, and yet there was an out-of-body feeling to it. I knelt over John for a long time, unconsciously praying so loudly that the little kids, who were huddled on the aft deck in Amelia's embrace, could hear me above the roar of sea. Then I walked up and down the swaying starboard deck in a daze while John remained pinned beneath the mast. I stopped time and again where he lay and where Ben sat in their blood trying to heave up the mast and free his father. The weight of it, the steel-cable tied-down tangle of it, was obviously impossible. Ben took trips back to the kids and to Amelia to assure them that everything was going to be okay. He was calm and assured, but with that great flow of blood still dripping down his face. Then he would come try again.

"Jean," John said to me, his teeth clenched in pain. "The other kids okay?"

"Okay?" I stared into the black sea. "Yes, everything's okay." I meant no sarcasm—we were so in God's hands that part of me had given up. I stroked his bloody hair. Good husband. Good man. Good father. Great lover. And moments ago he was standing so handsome in the doorway of our stateroom, which was now awash with laptop computers and DVDs and clothing and a thousand things that would soon slide down a mile into the deep.

I went forward and stood in the darkness at the tip of the starboard bow. I was not helping much. I was in shock—all but the fainting; there was no good place to faint. I had lost control of my body and my mind, as happens at such times.

Ben was frightened, but he had his fear in hand. He was doing things; I was impressed. His father was pinned to the bouncing deck, sometimes screaming in pain and sometimes praying aloud. The tourniquet was helping, but he was still bleeding badly because of the kneading motion of the mast. The mast. The mast. The mast. Impossible to lift.

Ben seemed to have done what I could not: accept that John was very likely not going to make it, and that the rest of the family needed leadership and help.

Ben and Amelia somehow understood that I was in shock. They made sure the small kids were in a safe place for now. They began to scavenge for more survival supplies. I was on their list: Get Mom functioning again.

[4]

AN IRRATIONAL CALM

Odd to see John like that in the dark water—so unlike him. He had always seemed to enjoy an arm's-length relationship with mortality. My confused mind was wondering why he was handling this so differently—stupid for him to be staying under the mast and drowning a little with each wave when his children and I were about to die for lack of some good plan from him.

Years before, as a young construction worker high inside the rising steel lattice of a new power plant's mammoth cooling tower, he had fallen. No one could possibly survive such a fall. I think of him free-falling backward, looking with interest at the clouds framed in the great circle of the tower. Einstein observed that a falling man feels no gravity. John landed on a small metal construction shed that was, by inches, in the perfect position to collapse and save him in its folding metal embrace. His coworkers watched as a helicopter raised him in a basket out of the tower's interior and into the sky. The men were sure he must be dead, and the wail of a siren that was used to mark another death at the project—

the dead whistle—sounded. From the slowly rising and rotating rescue basket, an arm appeared and John flipped a finger to assure his friends that life was still good. He was home that night with only bruises, having sneaked out of the hospital and stopped at a hamburger joint with his brother.

Porsches and vans and motorcycles have flown off curves, crashed sideways into trees, slipped through inches of safety, and he has largely brushed himself off after the firemen have pried open the steel to let him out. A coma or two, a repaired knee or so, but nothing to really slow him down or make him the least fearful of life.

Somehow I saw all that when I first met him. I didn't see him as foolhardy, for I would not have been attracted to that—but he was fearlessly alive, living in a state of constant amazement.

I was living at the time in Westchester County in a New England–style farmhouse surrounded by trees on a country road. I sold advertising in a newspaper Sunday supplement. John was living in Greenwich Village. He had recently been building and selling boats in the Caribbean. He and some friends came up to Westchester County to visit a mutual friend. John's humor, I think, was the thing, his confidence in the world, a sense that life is grand—an adventure beautiful beyond words. He saw me staring at that in him; he saw me staring at someone not afraid to free-fall, not afraid of the deep—someone who understood the shallows to be the greater danger to our lives.

He had a girlfriend at the time, and I had a boyfriend, but our attraction was total. We went to dinner some weeks later to sort it out. The restaurant was an hour-and-a-half drive away from anyone we knew. Fate is not subtle when it is serious. We were seated in the same small dining room where John's girlfriend happened to be dining with her secret paramour. It was all very friendly. We finished our meals and behaved admirably, all of us. But John and I were, from that night forward, a couple. The wedding, a small affair at a yacht club on the mainland side of Long Island Sound, was watery and beautiful.

Before we met we had both been creatures of the Caribbean. I had assistant-managed a charter sailing service in the Virgin Islands. John built, sailed, and sold boats. Later he imported building materials to the islands. The island life had worked itself deep into John's bones. Even as a young boy, he had his eyes always on the sea, looking for ways to work on boats. But you get to a certain age and you have to make a decision: If you stay in the Caribbean, you might become one of the too-tan sand crabs aging in the rum bars and charter docks of that ever-young, ever-inebriated world. Or you can go home to make your fortune and return with a fine boat and the resources to live well in paradise—and from there perhaps you can explore the world by way of all its seas. For John, that was it. He came home to finish college and make his fortune. He never thought for a moment that he would not return to the sea some-day. As for me, I knew I wanted a long and meaningful life of explora-tion and adventure, but I was through with the luxurious dissipation that island living can become after your midtwenties. I wanted a life and a family.

Our courtship and the early years of our marriage were green and lovely—the memories stay with me every day: Ireland, where we went for a time after our wedding, with John hitched us a morning ride on a horse-drawn milk wagon. All we wanted to do was snuggle and neck, but the tweedy, old, pipe-smoking deliveryman wanted to educate us a wee bit regarding, don't you know, the peat-cutters' strike that threatened the warmth of every blessed Christian cottage in County Cork. We didn't need peat to keep warm. The breakfast hills around us, so rained-upon and emeraldine, couldn't have been greener had we taken some psyche-delic, nor could we be more hungry for each other. I remember watching sheep being loaded from some quay, listening to the sea there, taking the wind into my hair—so long and honestly golden then. I remember bur-rowing into his wool layers—his coat, sweater, and sash, digging for a wee bit of chest to kiss or maybe bite.

We found ourselves soon enough in the grassy hills of Southern Cali-

fornia raising children. John's construction experience and his fearless-
ness led him to a successful career building homes near the sea with his
brother. At sunset, I would often see him looking across the landscape as
if the grassy hills and ravines might be the swells and troughs of a rolling
sea. Just beyond the hills were the curves and mists of the ocean itself, always pulling his eyes to the horizon. He could never pass up a good
painting of a fine ship or a good book about sailing. Our walls and book-
shelves were filled with them. I knew the second act of his seafaring days
would announce itself one day, and this other shoe—deck shoe—would
drop. When the housing market tumbled and our savings dwindled,
John started drinking—his dream was drifting out of his reach. But he
dealt with his problem, went to his meetings, and we hung on until the
market turned upward again. I quit my insurance job and set up a home
office to make his contracting business as successful as we both could
make it. As our fortunes improved and he passed his fiftieth birthday, I
knew he was fast approaching the now-or-never moment. A good part-
ner needs to have an eye out for such things and be ready to say yes.
He was too good a father and too precious a mate for me to treat his
dreams otherwise. And his dreams had become mine, just as mine had
become his.

John took me down to the San Diego Harbor to catch a ride on a new
catamaran, just to show me how smoothly this kind of boat sails. If a regular sailboat rides something like a motorcycle, a "cat" rides like a limou-
sine. It doesn't "heel over" sideways in the wind like a regular sailboat.
This means the kids don't slide off the decks into the water, and it means
you can cook and otherwise live a life while you are crossing the sea. It
won't capsize unless you beg it to—by, say, running with full sails in a
hurricane. It won't easily capsize because its width, called its beam, is
over half the length of its twin hulls. The absence of a heavy keel makes it
nearly unsinkable—this was the biggest selling point for me. Being so
"beamy," to use the sailors' term, makes the boat a real pain to bring in to

dock, and very few marina boat slips are wide enough for it. But the trade-offs, safety and stability, are worth the trouble—and a catamaran is a rocket in a stiff wind.

On that same sparkling morning of our first ride, we met a Santa Barbara family with small kids who had been living on a cat for six months, seeing the world and loving it. Their six-year-old and twelve-year-old both told me they were learning so much and having a great time. I suddenly felt that our own kids were captives to a dull and artificial life, while the beauty of the real world was passing them by.

For myself, I was certainly tired of the ever-faster treadmill, and I knew there was a Garden of Eden out there—I had seen it as a young woman. I worried for the kids—about uprooting them and exposing them to the dangerous life of the sea. I worried what it would do to me. The seafaring woman we met looked as though she had probably once been a regular customer of the salons and stylish boutiques of Santa Barbara, but the sea had taken her a bit: Her nails were untidy; her hair was growing out gray where it had probably been colored before. The sun at sea is hard on your skin if you become careless about sunblocks and hats and such—it had taken hers some. I didn't want that for myself. I was who I was; I liked my hair and my nails and my face and figure just so. It was hardly the center of my life, but it was important to me. It was a concern. But I knew I could figure that out. I could figure a lot of things out, if it meant seeing Eden again and taking our children there.

On John's fifty-first birthday, he received a little envelope from me with airline tickets for the two of us to go to the big Miami International Boat Show and look around.

The children, so enmeshed in school activities and their budding social lives, were worried the minute they sniffed this salt. *Why are Mom and Dad going to the big Florida boat show?* How weak and useless I must have looked to them, bending to the will of this monster Ahab who, only days earlier, had been a kindly father driving them to their games, ballet lessons and surf-team practice. Now he was spreading brochures about faraway island paradises over their schoolbooks as they tried to study. He was intent on capturing this thing he had seen earlier in life, and now he had a crew—a slave crew, in the minds of these young Californians. Compulsion! One can only pray it is a compulsion for life and beauty instead of death and destruction. I hoped it would be the learning opportunity of a lifetime for each of the kids—not some cruelty where we were taking them unfairly away from their chums and their school days. They would have to decide later in their own lives whether or not it had been worth it.

It took a few years of preparation to make the adventure as safe as possible and to prepare for their long-distance schooling. I worried mostly about the water itself; it was the thought of the kids drowning that sold me on choosing the unsinkable catamaran, and it was the nightmare of a child falling overboard that made me insist that John build a low net fence all around the deck.

Everybody knew how to swim. Everybody wore his or her vest on deck when we were under way. Everybody watched everybody when near the water. When we'd had to outrun pirates and chase druggy Jack Sparrow types off the boat early in the trip, it was the kids we worried about, not ourselves. But here it was John who was dying, drowning. I had never figured on losing him. Not in my wildest. Shooting him, maybe, but not losing him to the sea. His sea.

"What is that passage? What is that passage from the Bible to calm the water?" I had asked little Jack some time earlier as we all looked at the terrible red teeth of coral in the churning sea around us. He had spent time at Sunday school, and I guess I asked him because he seems to remember everything. I was trying to remember the story told in Matthew, Luke, and Mark: "A squall came down on the lake, so that the boat was being swamped, and they were in great danger. The disciples went and woke Him, saying, 'Master, Master, we're going to drown!' He got up and rebuked the wind and the raging waters; the storm subsided, and all was calm. 'Where is your faith?' he asked his disciples."

Where was our faith? It came quickly with our fear. We began to pray aloud, the children and I. Ben was up front praying with John. We had been praying to ourselves and some aloud from the very first, from before the mast had come down like an angry war club, the first and quite unwelcome answer to our prayers. We are Catholic, so our prayers are the short "Our Father" and "Hail Mary" variety, though we added our personal words more and more until only our deepest thoughts survived.

So unfair, I thought. That very spot on the deck where John now suffered was the exact spot where, nearly every night, he prayed in what he thought was total privacy. But it was right above the little kitchen in the starboard hull, and if you got up in the middle of the night and went into that galley for a little bite, and if you hit the time right, you might hear him through the skylight hatch. He would have already done his push-ups in the cockpit, maybe five sets of twenty, before heading to his place on the starboard deck, where he so beautifully expressed his gratitude for being in this very big, incredibly beautiful world, and for having all of us in his life and with him now. It was lovely to close my eyes and listen to him. And in that very same spot he should be struck down? I am not a fan of such cruelty.

John was in the dark there now, bleeding, praying aloud for the safety of his family and for forgiveness for his life. Ben, by glow stick, was struggling with the mast—we'd all joined him in that impossible effort for a time. He was asking his father's forgiveness for being a teenager. Amelia was comforting the kids, first in the salon and later on the port deck, and I was standing on the bow, staring into the dark sea, thinking mostly about drowning, which had always been my worst fear for myself and especially for the kids—I had countless nightmares about their drowning in a pool or a bathtub. Now it was entirely possible they would all drown this night, this hour. I thought about my selfish attitudes and felt remorse for being so, so imperfect in life and now in death. Just standing there. I told God that, if he would let us survive this night, then I would make it mean something worthwhile.

And then, somehow I felt calmer than I have ever felt. Unreasonably so. Irrationally so. I looked over the scene of our wrecked life and understood that somehow whatever was supposed to happen was going to happen. This is what it is. This is who we are. This is where we are. We are a struggling life-form on this reef. Look at us. This is what happens on this planet. We are of it. It ends when it ends, and it is a beautiful show, a great adventure. This is how we live and die. I smiled—a crazy smile for sure—and I looked through the dark at the mad beauty of it.

I had been set on learning how to scuba dive at the beginning of our journey, back in Saint Thomas. Once underwater, making the tank work for me, looking at the incredible beauty of the coral and the fish, the sea of underwater grass, my own family like fish around me, I suddenly felt more a part of the planet than I had ever experienced. Floating in colors and warm sea, every creature smiling a big smile. Well, if I were to go down tonight, drowning might be uncomfortable, but that would take, what, fifteen seconds? Then I would be floating down there in all that beauty and becoming part of it. Fine. Then I looked around and decided that, well, it's also natural for life to struggle to survive, so let's have a little of that.

If a change of tide or a rogue wave dragged the boat seaward, it would take only seconds for the *Emerald Jane* and John to slide off the coral shelf into the mile-deep ocean. John was lashed to the white boat as surely as Ahab was tangled to his great whale—and would go down just as surely.

John was thinking of the life raft, still tangled in lines near the bow. It needed to be free in case the boat slipped into the deep. It needed to be ready. John grabbed Ben's arm hard and screamed in his ear, "You've gotta free up the raft, so it's ready. Ben, listen to me, if the boat goes, I don't want the raft pulled down with her; make sure you've cut all the lines

holding the raft. Put it here on the deck and fasten it with loose hitches."
Hitches are secure but they can be untied as quickly as shoelaces.

John could see that Ben understood.

"If the boat slips farther down the reef, get everyone in the raft and
keep it from getting snagged by the rigging or anything as the boat goes
down. And, Ben, you know, if there's time, come work this knife into my
knee joint to free me. It is just like poppin' a turkey joint, but it will take
all your strength. I'll pass out, but don't worry about that." John doesn't
ordinarily think so crudely, but he was searching for a way to help Ben's
mind find a way to do this. He had to dehumanize his leg.

John waited for Ben's answer. "We'll deal with that problem later if it
comes up, Dad. We're going to get you outta here."

With that, Ben turned and went off to another task.

"Mom," Ben called. "We're going to need your help." He was standing
beside me. He smiled warmly and put his hand on my arm. Dear God, we
need better coming-of-age ceremonies in our culture. This was too hard,
but it was that: Ben had become an adult in this hour. I followed him
back to the aft, where the two younger kids were calm under Amelia's
care. I stopped to be with John for a moment. He said I should bring the
kids to talk to him before too long—before maybe it was too late.

[5]

WHOSE FAULT?

Ben and I thrashed through the waves and debris to cut and untangle the thicket of rigging cables, but each wave seemed to re-lash John and his mast to the deck. I finally went aft to see to the kids.

Amelia had wisely put Jack in charge of holding the emergency beacon. The signals to distant satellites, and the GPS signals that would allow the beacon to report our position, were all too weak to work reliably in this remote area, but the little yellow cylinder was nevertheless our only remaining hope of rescue. Jack held it as reverently upright as an altar boy with a chalice. The little guy who had been in a panic in the first terrifying moments was now showing his considerable grit, worried more for his pet turtle than for himself. Speedy was safe in his lap.

Jack is a pure creature of nature. The first time I saw him with a wild creature was in our garage in California. He was swinging a snake around his head like a lasso. That was the first snake. For the second snake he begged to have a terrarium in the house. The compromise was that the glass box would be kept in the garage. It was empty before the first day was over; the snake was lost somewhere in the house. It showed up days later in a basket of dirty laundry being loaded into the washer. Frogs, snakes, bugs, just seem to line up outside waiting for Jack. On our voyage, he might as well have been a sea creature himself—always diving deep and popping up with something in his hands. Once it was a fairly large octopus, which you have to hold just so. He had learned how to do that from someone along the way. Any fish, any creature of any kind, Jack would rattle off the name of it and something interesting about it. We would later look it up and see that he had been exactly right. He tried to make friends with a sea lion that instead chased him across a rocky shore.

Jack cannot just come into a room. He bursts in. He comes in to get things moving. He would tease little Camille about something—tickling her or taking away a toy, claiming it was his own just to get her going. I asked him why he did this and he said that it was just too much fun not to. So then Ben would come in and yell at Jack, because Ben has always been Camille's guardian angel. Camille would be crying and Jack laughing and Ben yelling. And then Amelia would come in and yell at Ben for making it worse, and Ben would shout at her to shut up, shut up, and then John would come in and get so mad that they were all fighting. Jack enjoyed setting all the family planets in motion in this way—a miniature Teddy Roosevelt charging up every hill and invading every country just for the glory of battle, perhaps because war is where life is most vividly set against the alternative, and Jack is pure life.

Just before the trip, he was diagnosed with a hip-bone disorder that required him to have surgery and be in a wheelchair for several months. I thought this would drive him insane, but he switched from Teddy to Franklin Roosevelt, impressing his schoolmates with his pitiful circumstances and coming home with their lunch treats and sometimes their lunch money. He makes every day a great show. When he screamed that he did not want to die, he did so because he knew how grand a thing life is.

Amelia was tortured by the sounds of her father suffering so. I took her forward, and we held his hands and comforted him. The sea washed over him again and again—he gasped "Okay" each time when it was over. His shivering was now severe, and he had to fight it to speak clearly. His hemorrhaging had slowed, but blood still flowed across the deck. In these first three hours, he would lose three-quarters of his blood, which should have killed him. And it would have done so had he not been too worried about us to leave us. Of that I am certain. Even so, kidneys begin to fail and the mind goes strange places. He knew he needed to speak to the little kids very soon.

Amelia carefully shepherded Jack and Camille forward along the bucking deck. Jack clutched the grail beacon to his chest. John gripped their freezing hands. He motioned with his eyes for Amelia and Ben to draw near.

"Listen to me, okay? If I go to sleep tonight, it's okay. If I'm sleeping, then nothing hurts me. If I'm asleep, I won't be freezing-cold like I am now. Okay?"

Camille and Jack did not understand the full meaning of his message. That was okay. It was meant to be understood after the fact.

John began to pray aloud a little crazily, maybe because, until this moment, he hadn't really accepted the idea that he was about to die.

"Father, I am a sinner, a most grievous sinner, through my fault, through my fault, through my most grievous fault!"

His mind was somewhere new. The pain had moved into dreamtime. A great sword, red hot from a great fire, hovered over him and then brushed along his leg. He clamped his teeth so tight with the pain that, in reality, vertical cracks began to grow in his teeth.

The blade penetrated, frying its way through his calf as he fought it. He fought this pain and this image until he could fight it no longer. A hideous scream came from his contorted mouth, his twisted face. He was ashamed to see the kids still near, horrified. He was broken. The blade found bone and his breath backed up his throat and froze there. Jack and Amelia's own contorted faces were above him, looking down on his racked body in disbelief. He saw their faces and then closed his eyes against that pain and against his own failure to be strong for them.

He began a quiet chant of prayers, his eyes closed and his body clenched.

"Father, take me but protect my wife and children." He was making an offering of his pain and his death, hoping it would be enough to negotiate the release of his family.

When the surges of pain came hardest, he abandoned his own words and returned to the prerecorded prayers of his faith: "Holy Mary, Mother of God, pray for us sinners now and at the hour of our death."

His eyes opened and rolled back; he looked into the foam of the next wave coming. We were helpless, unable to help him. Amelia took the kids to the safer port-side deck, where they huddled.

"Big one," Ben shouted, reaching down to hold John while a high breaker swept the deck. When John's face reemerged from the foam, he was still praying, "... protect the lives of my wife and my children."

"I'm sorry," he said close into my ear. Sorry for leaving us? Sorry for wanting this trip? It didn't matter. I kissed his forehead.

———

He had nothing to be sorry for that I didn't share. We had done this together, and we had tried so hard to do it right. We bought this used cat because it was the safest big boat we could find in our range—about the price of a very small, fixer-upper suburban house.

There were better boats for sale—bigger, air-conditioned, full-dishwasher kinds of boats that broke my heart. But they weren't necessarily safer, and we could fix this one up. It would be great. We installed homework desks and other modern conveniences for our planned year of living in the real world. John shanghaied us for shakedown cruises and taught us, quite literally, all the ropes so we could sail safely anywhere. One of the practice runs took us all the way down to Key Largo, where we ran into Jack's basketball coach from California—sailing is exactly like that: The small world gets smaller and cozier, with little parties aboard at sunset.

When the day finally came to leave California, when the kids had packed their bags, said goodbye to friends and teachers, and made their last useless protest that we were ruining their lives, we headed to the East Coast where the *Emerald Jane* awaited. We let a recently divorced friend and her kids have our house while we were away. She would pay our utilities and our lawn service and forward our mail. This way, our kids didn't have to throw all their things overboard—we just had to make some room in the closets.

We were soon looking out my sister's window at a great storm on Long Island Sound. Hurricane Isabel had swept up from the Carolinas to New England. John babysat the boat, moored below in the Sound, while the children and I waited safely in Jane's sturdy house.

John worried that the mooring might not be strong enough; he stayed on board, ready to start the engines if the boat was blown toward shore.

If you were looking at the *Emerald Jane* from up on the hill, you could see how long and wide it was: The two hulls, fifty-five-feet long, white with a few lines of green trim. From a distance, it usually looked quite grand, especially under its eight-story sail puffed full of wind. But as the hurricane blew into Long Island Sound, our battened-down boat far below us looked tiny and fragile—a child's toy of cork and paper.

John held the boat together that night by sheer will. Rain came like a waterfall. The boat swung violently back and forth; John pulled himself through the blast and deluge to secure lines and hatches and tighten all the equipment stored above deck. He then somehow fixed a pot of coffee and watched the show all through the night. He will probably be able to fix a pot of coffee on Judgment Day.

Staying on the boat through the storm was a simple act of love. The relationship of a sailor to a boat is quite personal. There is something deeply archetypal at work: The sea, of course, is the feminine spirit, womb of life, smoother of rough edges, enclosing, nurturing, sometimes lying down in peaceful beauty and sometimes ruthless.

And the ship is the sacred vessel, the grail, within which the sacrifice of a sailor's days and nights, and maybe a sailor's life itself, are offered. The ship, in some mystical and romantic way, represents life itself to the sailor.

And, if the boat is all that, then the mast is . . . well, the mast is the mast and ours was the biggest in nearly any harbor. John took pride in how big the thing was: eight stories. Coming back from some land excursion, it was always easy to find our boat in any crowded marina. That mast meant speed and power.

A fine sailboat is the disciplined product of thousands of years of sailing wisdom. Things learned five thousand years ago are reflected in her every elegant curve and fastener. Most remarkably, she is able to take the frontal attack of the wind and turn it to her favor—a martial move.

A beautiful boat is a physical aid to meditation, a machine for finding wisdom, a calculator and divining device for answering any great question: logic made visceral to help you think through anything as you sail along. And her beauty? Beauty gives energy to men—more than they can handle sometimes. Her youth is in her smooth lines, her scent and moisture, her desire for adventure under a strong captain, the curve of the wind in her great triangles of canvas.

The *Emerald Jane*, I knew very well, was the other woman in our relationship. I felt a little jealous at first, but as John's youthful enthusiasm came back to him through her, I was the beneficiary. And so I also came to love her, despite his constant attentions and expenditures and his incessant, boyish praise of her.

It did not, therefore, seem odd to me when, cleaning behind a cabinet on the boat, I found a note tucked there by John during the early days when he was still improving and testing the boat and I was far away in California with the kids. It was like a prayer tucked into the Wailing Wall. It was a love note to this *Jane,* who would become such an important member of our family. Indeed, every repair bill, every costly improvement, was because "she needs a new..." or "she'll be happier if we upgrade the..." The note was a simple expression of feelings. It complimented the ship for her beauty and speed. The note promised that she would be cared for with great love. The note expressed hope and trust that she would, in turn, take her new family to see the beauty of the world and return us all safely. I tucked it back where I found it and didn't say a word, as I knew very well, and long before I found the note, that John had a thing for the *Emerald Jane* and that was the way it was going to be. But reading it was deeply moving to me in very complex ways.

You will think the note thing a little strange unless you have lived long with a sailor of your own, or are yourself one of these creatures. I am not suggesting that marinas are littered with such notes; every sailor shows this love in his or her own crazy way.

And what of the other side to love? How would this *Jane* react when she gleaned that the captain was going to just dump her on the market in Australia when he was through with her—when he had used up the best years of her life? What, in her fury, might she do to her captain and his precious little family? These kinds of thoughts are not outside a sailor's watery worldview.

In the calm of the dawn, the damage in Long Island Sound was visible everywhere: A boat moored nearby had capsized and sunk; a power cruiser was sideways on the beach. The *Emerald Jane* was fine. John was exhausted, but the night's adrenaline, which had given the kids and me serious second thoughts about the whole project, had only turned up his spark. He went about making a few more last-minute improvements, and then it was time.

"Let's get everything on board," he said. "C'mon. This is your captain, speaking. Move it."

The kids moaned and looked at me, hoping for some hint of salvation.

"He's a queer man, Captain Ahab—so some think—but a good one. Oh, thou'lt like him well enough; no fear, no fear. He's a grand, ungodly, god-like man, Captain Ahab; doesn't speak much; but, when he does speak, then you may well listen. Mark ye, be forewarned; Ahab's above the common; Ahab's been in colleges, as well as 'mong the cannibals; been used to deeper wonders than the waves; fixed his fiery lance in mightier stranger foes than whales. His lance! aye, the keenest and the surest that out of all our isle! Oh! he ain't Captain Bildad; no, and he ain't Captain Peleg; he's Ahab, boy; and Ahab of old, thou knowest, was a crowned king!"

"C'mon guys," I said, leading them down the hill to the water.

Well, here it is. Take a look around as the kids, John, and I pack in our luggage and supplies.

The *Emerald Jane* is a fair-sized catamaran, meaning a double-hulled sailboat. The twin hulls are stuffed with five little staterooms and four tiny bathrooms, called heads, plus a small but efficient galley and our navigation station. The hulls are joined together by an upper deck that includes an enclosed salon with slanted windows facing forward and to the sides. It's rather like an enclosed raft placed on two huge canoes, with the staterooms and galley in the canoes.

From down in either of those hulls, you step up a small stairway into the salon, about eight-by-fifteen feet, which has a large, golden-brown wraparound sectional couch, a chart table, and a folding table for indoor meals and for projects and homework. The aft wall of the salon has a sliding glass door that goes out to the ten-by-fifteen-foot aft deck, called the cockpit, which is covered with an emerald-green canvas awning called a bimini. Under the bimini is a built-in table where we eat our family meals in good weather.

At the far aft end of the cockpit are twin steering wheels. You have one wheel on each side of the stern so you can have a clear view whether the sails are on the left or right. Also, coming into port, you will want to be steering from the side of approach, as the boat is so wide. The canvas bimini sits a little higher than the roof of the salon so you can see through the gap—under the bimini and over the salon—to steer the boat. If that isn't enough visibility for you, there is a square hole in the bimini right above the wheel area. You can stand up on the tool locker behind you and see over everything. In bad weather, you button up the bimini with flexible plastic windows.

Ben and Jack's rooms, because they are in the very tips of the two hulls, are rocking places when in high seas or under full speed. If it gets too much for them, they can sleep on the sofas up in the salon.

The connecting salon and deck between the twin hulls are high enough to allow the sea to run underneath the boat between the hulls. A double winch on sturdy stainless cranes—davits—at the stern of the boat holds our dinghy up out of the water. That little motorboat is our shuttle when we're anchored off a beach or out in the middle of a harbor. Up front, a green cross-webbed safety net extends between the twin bows like a trampoline, and our inflatable life raft is stored up there in a deep locker.

There was a mix of excitement and disgruntled dismay as we loaded her up.

I was letting John take the rap for this, but it wasn't just John's dream. I had been watching my children's lives at a distance. I had too many errands to run, too many car pools and team practice times and appointments. Helping to run our construction business was a full-time job, too. My two youngest had recently complained that I never played with them. I realized that I really didn't know how to do that. My family dream was slipping out from under me—I was a stranger in my own house, too distracted to have any real life with them.

My mother was a busy professional woman—a nurse with six kids at home. The time I remember loving her most was when she took me out on Lake Valhalla in Upstate New York—just the two of us floating there, fingers tracing in the cool summer water. That moment has stayed with me. She is the "Jane" in the boat's name. Calling the boat after her gave me the feeling that her spirit was traveling with us—she had died of cancer ten years earlier. We renamed the boat using the traditional rechristening ceremony: a sprinkling of champagne and an announcement to Poseidon—mythical god of the sea—of the name change, and declarations shouted in four directions to the four winds. It is considered very bad luck to change a boat's name without the proper ceremony.

John wanted to sail the endless, lonely sea, but I wanted to explore the ports and the people. I wanted my life of adventure to get moving before my life was over. I wanted my children to step off the treadmill of designer jeans and obscenely expensive sweet-sixteen parties. It was not just John who wanted to go.

On September 22, 2003, we were all aboard and heading south down Long Island Sound to Manhattan. We passed the point of turbulence into the East River, with John pretending some difficulty with the "treacherous" current of Hell Gate, just to tease the kids. We cruised alongside the breathtaking New York skyline. Here is where I had lived many of my younger years. Here is where John and I had prowled the restaurants of the Village and the East Side. When you live in the City you see those big sailing ships out there, and maybe you dream. But, dear God, by whatever fate or fortune, it was *us* out here now—and blessed with such a beautiful family on the deck beside us. To the hard-dreaming Manhattan men and women no doubt looking at us from that working Monday's far windows and shores, I sent my wishes that they would have their turn, too—their bright moment on the water.

We passed near the Statue of Liberty, slid under the Verrazano Bridge, and then headed out to sea on a southerly course, the Jersey Shore off to starboard. We were finally doing this thing, and on such a beautiful day.

With sunset, the light breeze fell away to a flat calm. A fog rolled across the water, thickening by midnight. John set the radar to eight miles and introduced Ben to its switches and dials—a video game where you absolutely have to win every time or else actually die. "Sweet," Ben said.

If John had sometimes been less than patient with Ben, there would be a wealth of great moments for them now.

At 3:00 a.m. John and Ben were still at it. Ben was learning to estimate the distance and speed of ships without the help of the radar—just by their running lights. He was picking it up. The *Emerald Jane* would need to swing wide to avoid running into a tug towing two barges in the dark. Ben got it right. He looked satisfied with himself. We sailed the next day into Baltimore Harbor.

John set about making last-minute improvements while the kids and I prowled the city and used book stores as study halls for schoolwork. I need to run as often as I can—I run every morning if there is a spit of land within reach by dinghy or dock. In Baltimore, I ran in a half-marathon and did all right—actually, a personal best. Then I went shopping.

I bought an emergency rescue satellite beacon. It was a new kind of GPS thing—a Pains Wessex Emergency Position Indicating Radio Beacon (EPIRB)—that I saw on a television talk show; the sailors interviewed had been saved by it. We had a rescue beacon on the boat, but it didn't broadcast GPS coordinates or family-contact information like this new one. John didn't like the price of it, but I really wanted it as insurance. Besides, we had spent far more on computer games for the kids.

Then it was John's turn to shop. He took our life raft in for inspection and discovered that it would not properly inflate. He came back with a brand-new Switlick raft that was bigger and cost as much as a month of dinners out. In fairness, since the old one wouldn't inflate properly, he had a point. But our little nest egg for this trip was starting to crack, and we weren't even on the high seas yet.

———

But on the reef, it was now that very life raft that might save us—and that emergency beacon. I peered across the wreckage to look for the comforting red light of it. There it was, safe in Jack's embrace.

We were still shouting over the crashing surf and the endless lurching of the boat. And yet there was an intimacy now—we seemed to know what each other was thinking; we might as well have been whispering.

"Mom," Ben said close to me as we held John, "I was really frightened. But now I feel somehow peaceful. Really peaceful, like on Christmas."

It was the feeling that had come over me earlier on the bow. So I said I understood. When my mother lay dying of cancer at a hospital in New York, my sister Carol and I had felt this profound peace as mom slipped away from her body. We felt it and we sensed that she felt it. My sister and I looked at each other and smiled. Is it the final little compensation for the tragic combination of self-awareness and mortality?

Whatever it was, it was preparing us to let John go in peace.

For the first time, I was calm enough and strong enough to look closely at John's injury.

"Mom, you don't want to see it. It's really bad." Ben said, but then he moved aside so I could see under the mast.

I was suddenly dizzy at seeing it—like some monster had bitten John's leg nearly off. I had the crazy idea of going belowdecks to find a medical book down there and some bandages, but Ben stood in front of me.

"No, Mom. I won't let you go down there." As he restrained me, a wave of incredible power burst through the windows of the salon. Those windows were all but bulletproof to resist even hurricanes, and yet they burst instantly under the wave—the salon flooding full in the same second or two. Had I been in there, the water and the great blades of the windows would have killed me.

I took a deep breath. We are going to get the mast off John's leg. We have to do that. This was all I could think.

Amelia and the little kids were inside the tent canopy of the life raft, now tethered on the deck next to John. Through the open flap, they could see and hear his pain. The three children prayed together, listening to John praying for them. Amelia was amazed through her tears that he prayed only for them and not for himself.

Ben scurried aft and salvaged chocolate bars from the outside cockpit fridge for his little brother and sister. Jack and Camille sat silently there, strong but deeply stricken—poster children for some awful something that was now our own life. Jack clung to the beacon and held it just so; his chin was painted in the red glow of its little light.

"What about my stuffed animals?" Camille suddenly cried. Ben assured Camille that her toys would find new homes with King Neptune and the mermaids. This sounded all right to her—not great, but all right considering the circumstances.

Amelia seemed so calm.

I think I worried for Amelia more than the other kids when we were planning the trip. She would just be coming into her teen years. How would it be for her without a crowd of friends? I had read charming accounts of cruising families meeting other cruising families. Their children would play in lovely ways with each other. Everyone would catch fish and turn in slow motion to smile at their parents, with drops of water flying off their swirling hair and cute noses. It certainly wasn't working out like that at first. At the beginning of the journey, as when we were in Baltimore still making repairs before heading to sea, we all had cabin fever, and she was no exception. The kids kept up with their homework and learned their deck chores only because there was little else to do. Ben and Amelia bickered over who would get the sunny sofa bench on deck. Tiny injustices became provocations for war.

When Amelia's expensive dental retainer became ammunition in one of these battles, disappearing under the water, John's soaring anger so frightened the children that he perhaps truly became the Ahab of their fears. Ben, chased down the Baltimore dock by this madman, spent the next day diving with mask and a scuba tank, unsuccessfully searching the mucky bottom for the retainer. It smiles down there yet.

We enjoyed Baltimore, but winter was approaching. In the first week of November 2003 we sailed south to Norfolk, where we prepared for the journey into the open sea. All the frustrations of our long repairs and all the testiness from bobbing endlessly in the harbor at close quarters disappeared as the big mainsail popped full of wind.

From Norfolk, I thought we should sail south, stopping in the Carolinas to visit some of my relatives, and then to Florida. From there we could make short hops eastward into the Bahamas and then all the way to the Caribbean.

John had never liked this idea. Sailing due east from Florida would take us right into the trade winds and the wind-driven ocean swell that fetches all the way across the Atlantic from Africa. John wanted to sail east to Bermuda—that would put the winds off our starboard, then sail south to the Caribbean with the winds off our port. It was either his long tack or my small ones. As we both had sailing experience, it was a friendly argument.

"The kids have never been out of the sight of land," I argued. "It's just too early in the voyage to expect them to handle the high seas in a little boat." Also I was frightened for myself.

"It's an adventure to go out there like that. It'll be a good way for them to get into the spirit of this," he argued back.

We arrived in Norfolk still at odds over the route ahead. Rounding the piers to enter the marina, we saw a graceful white ketch flying the British flag. The mast of this storybook sailing ship was taller than our own. Painted on the bow was a playful line of smiley-faced lemons and oranges under the craft's name, *Fruity Fruits*. We passed the binoculars around, laughing at the zany name of this gorgeous ship.

A woman from the marina took our lines as we nudged up to the pier. Handing off the boat was no small thing: I had tossed the lines short when we were learning to crew the boat in Long Island Sound. Ben had once overthrown, nearly knocking a fellow down with a fist of rope to his chest. Now we could hit our marks, and John could swing the boat in smoothly at just the right angle.

"Oh, good," the dock woman said. "You've got children. So do the Van Zwams on *Fruity Fruits*. They've got twins: a boy and a girl, thirteen."

So this was God saying maybe this is going to work out. My fantasy of meeting other sailing families, of the kids having interesting friends who were also exploring the world, could come true yet. Maybe the Van Zwams were heading our way.

John grabbed the boat's papers and went to sign in at the marina office.

"C'mon, Amelia, Ben." He was going to play matchmaker right then. Fine.

As they came near the *Fruity*, a pretty teenage girl with sun-bleached, braided hair came on deck. This would be Stephanie.

"Hollo," she said with a British lilt. "Would you like to come aboard?"

Amelia and Stephanie took about a minute to bond and were off giving each other tours. Our Ben and their Jason were not far behind. The parents, Steffan and Carolyne, both in early middle age, were soon on our deck visiting. Steffan, tall with a big stack of wavy black hair and a lean, princely face, had been raised in South Africa; Carolyne, a good-looking woman about my own age, was equal parts French and English. They had sailed *Fruity Fruits,* a first-class, sixty-seven-foot sailing yacht, across the Atlantic.

When you first meet such people, you of course wonder how they manage to spend their days sailing the world in a yacht. Are they trust-fund children of some industrial fortune? Are they financial robber barons on the lam from their home country? Did they win some lottery or lawsuit? Or, more like us, have they scratched their whole working lives for this moment, and have they sunk their every bit of savings and credit into their floating Winnebago? You mustn't ask, of course. You must let it come out in conversation. The Van Zwams seemed quite used to all this. They seemed born to a yachting life. South Africa—don't they have diamond and gold mines there? De Beers and Krugerrands and all that? I waited for the conversations that would reveal their situation— not that it mattered to us, of course, as their good company was what we cared most about. That they should have boy and girl twins the right age to pal around with our older kids was priceless. But, if you care, it was diamonds.

John recruited princely Steffan to lobby me regarding our route to the Islands: Bermuda was indeed the best way, he insisted—he had British Admiralty weather data rolled under his arm to prove it. I happened to know that weather data is wrong about as often as it is right. This fine-looking man sealed the deal, however, when he said they also happened to be going exactly that way.

"Think of it!" he said, clinking our glasses. Indeed.

And with that, the *Emerald Jane,* the *Fruity Fruits,* and their crews headed into deep water. It was a five-day trip. The first day was beautiful. The remainder was a horror—the roughest sea ever encountered even by the veteran Van Zwams—waves two stories tall all around us in a strong gale. The children, passed out from seasickness sedatives, were on the floor here and there next to their sloshing buckets. The soup I tried to make for dinner went flying across the salon. The sleeker *Fruity Fruits* lost us in the confused seas. Although our catamaran was solid against the wild sea, mean waves came up under the drumlike bottom of the salon as real explosions, sending us nearly to the ceiling every few seconds—an endless three days and nights. Winds from the northeast were opposing the great Gulf Stream drift of the sea, creating the high waves. The hazardous condition accounts for many of the lost ships blamed on the so-called Bermuda Triangle.

What would have been a difficult adventure years ago for twentysomething me was now a nightmare for fortysomething me. What a mistake, and we had just begun! Our California home was committed to others for a year or more. Our money was sunk into this vomit-soaked tub. We were stuck. I was seasick and depressed and had barely missed being seriously scalded by a flying kettle of boiling soup. This first leg was nine hundred long miles.

But John? Big sea, big smile. He was back there hanging on to the wheel, the salt blast combing his hair sideways like a rock star. Couldn't be happier. The sea was his personal roller coaster. *Emerald Jane* arrived in Bermuda eighteen hours ahead of *Fruity Fruits*.

Bermuda was beautiful, as it always is. Little Jack pronounced the villages way cool, and Amelia pulled out her sketch pad and pastels. It was the beginning of her new life as an artist and designer.

"The water is like air," she said, looking deep into the water and seeing every fish and rock, forever down deeper. Jack would, of course, soon be down there with the creatures.

Ben and his Dad would get a little rough with each other in the days after that. John and I would get a little rough with each other. Things would start to fall apart. Paradise is always the hardest place to be happy.

But even in the worst of all that, it was nothing like his suffering now on the dark deck. All those hard days seemed like paradise compared to this.

A shivering seizure overtook him, cracking his teeth a bit more.

John felt himself as two people now. He was mostly the inner man, watching his family proudly—watching Ben take charge. He could hear himself crying out in pain, could hear himself praying, but that was the old John way out there. The new John was getting ready to take a trip. Tranquillity slowly warmed him. The stars jittered above. This was the natural order of things on the reef. He thought about the pain he had put everyone through back in the Caribbean, but then he forgave himself for that. People are supposed to have problems.

It seemed the new John had some friends. He heard distinct voices. They were mocking in tone, hardly divine. "No reason to be cold, my son," the voices crooned in scornful, discordant tones. "Comfort is so close, and you so richly deserve it. Your injuries are grievous, and you've borne them well. Rest is your due." The mocking tone became soothing. "Let go now. Don't feel guilty. Everything is out of your hands now, so rest. Close your eyes for a moment and rest. Let go—why be so cold? Relax."

The deck already felt softer to him. Warmth crept gradually through him, and his manic shivering subsided. The salt no longer burned his eyes. Under the foam of the next wave, he felt himself breathing in the water.

No. Not ready. He forced himself up on his elbows, coughing out a lungful of water. He was not going to be talked out of his life by some sweet-talking spirits he had never met. This was all too familiar; all too much like the urge to have a drink. Dying would be the ultimate escape, and he wasn't going to leave his family like that again.

[6]

THE THING ABOUT DAD

John did almost leave us once. I sort of pushed him off the boat—not exactly, but he ended up in the water just the same. It was a particularly bad evening. He had been drinking. I guess I did push him.

John is the kind of man who lives in the moment. When he is not up to his ears in some great experience, he is dying, self-destructing. He is not good at waiting and planning, because those things are about the future. When things slow down, when everything shifts to a waiting mode, he's in trouble. Under the mast, he was having a pure experience, but he was also waiting. I didn't know if the pain would save him or the waiting would kill him.

Years ago, when the housing market slumped and he was just standing around waiting for it to return, his self-destruct mechanism kicked in. He started drinking. He drank as a young man, and he drank in his early sailing years in the Caribbean, but not in a problem sort of way, and not since. His drinking in California almost ended very badly. I had packed up the car with baby Ben's crib and stroller and was about to come inside and grab Ben when John suddenly understood what was happening and came outside to talk to me. His plea was so deep and beautiful that I relented. He helped me unpack, and he did get help right then—signed up for a meeting on the phone. We were intensely intimate that afternoon; we started over as lovers.

He stuck with AA and had been dry for over a decade by the time we began our voyage. I thought his drinking was ancient history. He still went to his meetings, which the kids thought were business meetings, but I had come to think that he so enjoyed those friendships, and so valued how he was able to help others, that he would never have another drink in his life. But maybe it was the pure experience of that community of AA friends in California that had kept him dry and happy. I was aware that the Caribbean is awash in social drinking, and is so far from his friends, but I also knew how he had been looking forward to this journey for so many years—he wouldn't want to blow it. And the kids! Such a big part of his parenting was modeling an iron-strong character for them.

As the first months at sea rolled by, I was more worried about our marriage and our family than about old issues like drinking. When we arrived at Bermuda after that wild passage, I was not happy. The kids were not happy. Ben, particularly, seemed to get more and more angry about being away from school and surfing. His relationship with John had its golden moments at sea, but sometimes he was downright bullying to little Jack and abusive to the rest of us. As little Jack never needed much provocation for war, a big, angry scene would often engulf all of us after Ben started something.

As soon as we sailed out of the storm into a calm and sparkling sunrise in Bermuda, we tried harder to find the beauty of our journey. Jack sat up at the wheel with his Dad that early morning as the Bermuda landfall grew on the horizon. John wanted to wake the rest of the kids, but he let them sleep. Finally, Jack went below and shouted from door to door that everyone was "missing the good stuff."

Mooring the boat stern-first against the dock in Saint George's small harbor was a tricky maneuver that was nevertheless flawlessly performed by our little crew. Ben even looked momentarily pleased.

John had everyone out snorkeling in the coral almost immediately, as the light was so spectacular. Camille saw a multicolored clown fish, and Jack spotted a moray eel slithering into a rocky lair. We later got to know the cobbled lanes and thatched-roof cottages of the village, which impressed the kids in a happy way I didn't expect. The native police constables in their starched Bermuda shorts and kneesocks smiled benignly. Little Camille gaped at them openmouthed as if they had stepped out of a storybook. Over the next few days, we kept up on schoolwork, explored the sea and land, and met the Van Zwams for an American-style Thanksgiving dinner aboard the *Emerald Jane*—I had brought a frozen turkey across from the mainland for this event. Preparing a full Thanksgiving feast in a galley about twice the size of an airplane restroom is, well, a Zen-like Houdini thing. The stress on me and John and the kids was a little too much, and some limited warfare broke out. But American Thanksgivings can be like that, and we were giving our South African friends the full show. The grand finale involved John going ballistic because Jack shot Ben in the head. Fortunately, it was with a soft-plastic pellet toy, but it might as well have been a bullet to the temple of Archduke Ferdinand: The war began.

Besides that bad evening, John and I just generally began to rub each other the wrong way about our different visions for the journey. He always wanted to move along to the next place if the present location wasn't a natural wonderland. If it was, he was content to stay and stare at it forever. I liked exploring, shopping, learning about new places, then I was ready to move on. Nature boy versus restless girl.

I would insist that we anchor near a shore where I could get in easily for a little morning run, and where I could watch the kids swim in and play. John wanted to anchor farther out where the boat was safer from the twists of shifting winds. Maybe I was always moving toward people and civilization, and he was always moving away.

The happy idea of being on a vacation will get you through the first few weeks, but after that it is just life in a very small, ever-bobbing house with an ever-changing neighborhood. And this wasn't meant as a vacation; it was meant as a great journey and maybe even a new way of life.

Everything is more difficult on a boat: Cooking is a juggling act; the toilets have to be pumped a dozen times per flush; there is no room for anything to be the least bit out of place. If you buy something, you must get rid of something. Doing the laundry for six people involves packing bags and going ashore and finding a laundry, or doing loads onboard, hanging things to dry, and praying it doesn't rain or blow too hard, sending the clothes into the sea. On board, everything breaks and must be repaired in some horribly expensive way. There is no place for anger to go except to the person in front of you. There are no teachers or coaches to share the load of education. I didn't know if we could manage—if I could manage. What was eating John was the slowness, the long layovers, the constant repairs that were sometimes beyond his mechanical abilities and would cost not only money but time, kid-arguing, time. Even doing the laundry was, as I said, a wasted half-day, when we used to just toss things into machines in the laundry room.

John was not having the kind of total stimulation he really needs; the present was pretty frustrating—everything waiting for some future resolution. That's when he falls apart. I could see some nervous something growing in his eyes and manner, and I didn't recognize what it was until too late.

There was another thing: Before we met each other, we had both spent time in Bermuda. We were now seeing places that had been important to us in our twenties. An old friend and I once had dinner with Teddy Tucker, the subject of Peter Benchley's *The Deep*. He showed me treasures from the sunken ships he had discovered. John had his own special-memory places. We were revisiting our pasts on bicycles and mopeds.

Maybe all this was somehow hard on us. We were confronting our lost youth, our mortality, our unlived lives.

The minute we had an open weather window, we were southward bound to the Caribbean— to Saint Martin in the French West Indies.

Saint Martin is a little south and east of the Virgin Islands. It would put us in good position to pick up some family members joining us onboard for the holidays. Saint Martin, a French anchorage, would be where we could finally buy an anchor chain to replace the one we had lost. *Emerald Jane* had been built in France, and only metric parts would work with some of her systems.

The journey to Saint Martin would be a thousand miles, with heavy seas at the outset. Unlike the crossing to Bermuda, the kids were traveling as real sailors now.

When he wasn't seasick, Jack practiced tying the bowlines and the hitches a little sailor needs to know. Ben was suddenly interested in how to "walk" a vessel's course across the map, correcting for magnetic variations. It was the kind of math that held his interest. Amelia's log entries from her watch were now well written with notes on wind speed and direction, compass readings and average knots.

These changes in the skills and attitudes of the crew should have cheered John, but they kind of rankled him. They did so because on board was a handsome sea salt named Derek, the former captain of the boat. We invited him along to join us for the passage from Bermuda to Saint Martin. He was a charmer of children, a knower of knots, a genius massager of necks. John was taking a backseat to his own dream. Derek taught the kids how to deep-sea fish with and without a pole—they caught wonderful mahimahi and he showed us how to clean and cook it just so. It was Derek who got Ben and Amelia interested in navigation.

Just the same, it was John's own navigation along an easterly curve that brought us to harbor in Saint Martin quite magnificently, and against the advice of Steffan Van Zwam and other captains. John had out-guessed them on the winds—though that did not spare us another hard, seasick passage in a seemingly endless gale. Even Derek got a little queasy. Not John.

The rest of us were soon laid low with an antinausea medicine that proved to be so strong that the boat looked like a morgue. We learned later that most sailors carry an antinausea pill called Stugeron, which is made for chemo patients but is sold in yachting ports around the world. It later worked well for us, killing the nausea without putting us under.

During that wave-crashing gale of a voyage, I made Ben and Amelia wear life jackets if they moved out on deck, even if they weren't on watch. I made the younger two wear theirs even in the more protected area of the cockpit. If the little ones wanted to leave the cockpit, they had to clip their safety tether to a stainless wire running across the deck. I made the two men do the same, though they hated agreeing to that. John didn't argue too much as Derek was aboard. Besides, nobody wanted to mess with me: I was nervous and moody and generally angry. This kind of sailing was not fun for me or the kids. John and Derek? Big smiles back there at the wheel, since the boat was really moving.

"We're in a groove now, buddy. This boat's going like she's on rails," John shouted over the waves and wind to Derek. Lurch, splash, lurch, splash, lurch, splash for a thousand miles. You try it.

John was out there every night, the sharp bows splashing the Atlantic water into a spray of diamonds under the moonlight. Knowing he was so in love with these moments, I couldn't be as angry as I wanted to be. I knew the peace he had come looking for was what I was seeing in his permanent smile.

"That's Alpha Centauri," he pointed out when it was calm enough one night for me to take him a coffee. Alpha Centauri happens to be

the nearest star to our solar system. It was rising above the horizon—
flashing like a beacon in jewel colors amid the glitter of the Milky Way.

These winds were the trade winds, blowing across from Africa just for
John now—finished taking their hurricanes westward for the season.

Saint Martin is a picture postcard: open-air markets with fresh
seafood, produce, and flowers spread along the waterfront; shaded lanes,
quaint homes, and small bistros with red-tile roofs necklaced along the
slopes; a French side and a Dutch side of the island make it unique.

After downing their breakfast cereal, the kids were in the water with
flippers and snorkels. If they'd been home in California on a December
day, their time would have been completely organized, from school hours
to piano lessons, sports, and homework. They were learning about some
things their own way now. There would be book study later, but the real
classroom today was underwater.

John and I were left to clean up the decks, coiling lines, making sure
the genoa jib was rolled tight and that the mainsail had folded into
proper pleats atop the boom. We hoisted the yellow Q (quarantine) flag
to indicate that we'd just arrived from foreign waters. In such a place, you
also hoist a French "courtesy flag," which just says you know where you
are and who's in charge. We couldn't find that flag. A port official arrived
by dinghy to remind us the courtesy flag was "de rigueur." We would buy
one in the village.

We had a small inflatable dinghy that the kids used. Early in our
stay, I had to run back to shore to retrieve a bag mistakenly placed in a
Dumpster—it had our laundry in it. The bag had vanished from the
Dumpster and the dinghy was soon gone from the dock where I left it.
I really needed a break from all this. I am a private, tidy person—a
planner—and all this was getting to me. John thought we needed to stick
around long enough to have the canvas bimini rebuilt; the struts that
held it up had proven to be too weak for open sea gales. The whole thing
was really too low—you had to duck to walk around in the cockpit and

we didn't have good visibility under it from the stern wheels. He found some yacht workers who said they could rebuild the struts and replace the green canvas. They dropped their cigarette ashes all over the boat.

I escaped with the kids and we explored the island and the villages of Marigot on the French side and Philipsburg on the Dutch side.

A week passed as the workmen tried and failed to correctly rebuild the bimini. We found a little church for our Sunday service, and introduced the kids to French tropical fare: baguettes and cheeses, pain au chocolat, rock lobsters, grilled bonito with lime butter. I was starting to feel my soul again; John was going crazy to be so stuck waiting for the workmen.

John and I ended up shouting over the location of our anchorage off Orient Beach. I had insisted we anchor close, and the wind almost blew the boat into the breakers. The kids were shocked to see us yelling. "Screw you" was my big bomb. The yachting life was turning me into someone I didn't like.

Something else about that very French beach: As we came ashore in the dinghy, we realized we were at a nude beach. The French are usually topless on all beaches but this one was total nudity for the whole family: moms, dads, grandmas, grandpas, and children running around. We kept our clothes on but enjoyed the water, until we saw the boat dragging. Jack was completely horrified by the lack of bathing suits; he sat on the beach almost the whole time with his hands to his eyes.

"Mom, I can't handle these Paris beaches," he said. Mr. Natural had his boundaries.

So the boat didn't like it either, and we made our scramble back and had our shouting match.

After we secured the boat farther out, John went back ashore to the little town along the beach. The grocery store where he gathered supplies had a shelf of half-pint bottles of rum, vodka—all of it. He looked but he didn't buy. We sailed onward.

The family crew seemed lazy to John—maybe because charismatic

Derek wasn't aboard. John was starting to think he was alone in the sailing part, which was the main part. He got snippy about people not doing their jobs properly. So, a little unhappily, we roared over the beautiful blue waves at nine knots as the grassy mounds of the British Virgin Islands slipped by on the horizon. The bimini, so badly repaired, was flopping in the wind. This, perhaps more than anything, was demoralizing John. The boat was a symbol of virginal perfection to him. She was tattered.

We had been on the boat for four months. Though we now lived inches from each other day and night, we had in many ways become more distant.

On Christmas Eve, we sailed into Saint Thomas. This was our old drinking territory. It had more homes, more sprawl now, but some old joints we knew from our twenties. Good Christmas shopping: a lobster snare for Jack—it was in his letter to Santa; new snorkeling fins for Camille. Yes, kids, Santa can find us. No, he doesn't need a chimney when he is visiting boats.

The bimini had become an obsession for John. We would stay in Saint Thomas as long as it took to fix it perfectly. He didn't want to go and he didn't want to stay; he hated that he had been so unable to fix things himself.

He felt tremendously apart from us. He worried that this dream trip was a humbug—that it wouldn't be the magic medicine to make our kids happily, ecstatically engaged with the beauty of the world, and that it wouldn't make all the fear and anger that had settled into my eyes over the years just wash away. Mortal reality was sitting heavily on his dreams this Christmas.

While the kids and I were wrapping presents, John wandered along the dock to a grocery store. I had sent him out to get the ingredients for our big Christmas dinner on board the next day. There they were again, the little half-pint bottles. He extended his arm, heavy as concrete, and picked up a vodka. Put it in the basket. His legs felt heavy, too, like the hard pull of a slow-motion nightmare with no escape. He was going to have that one little thing. We were so distant from him, so uncaring for the spirit of this great thing, that he might as well have a drink with someone he knew and could talk to about such things—his old self.

Locked in our head, he took two long pulls from the little bottle and felt at ease for the first time in a very long time. He had played the family game as well as he knew how for as long as he could. He just wanted this little break.

He poured half the bottle down the drain, filled the bottle with tap water, and let it slide into the sea from the porthole. Twelve years of sobriety. Not so bad, he figured: one nip every dozen years. The next day was Christmas and he was swimming in guilt, though I did not see it. Maybe I wasn't seeing him much at all.

John decided to reinforce the metal skeleton of the bimini himself. He found the metal and a man to help him. He found a good canvas shop in town. He worked for days while the kids and I snorkeled and explored. Ben found a paintball war jungle in the hills above town. We came and went, living our resort life, while John worked like our hired man. The bimini was coming along, but his spirits were falling.

One evening, we all jumped ship for a cheeseburger ashore. John said he wanted to stop at a hardware store—he told me to go ahead and order him a burger. When we were around the corner, he ducked into a market. He bought a little flask of rum. He had one sip in an alley. After dinner, I said I was exhausted and wanted to get back to the boat, but that anyone else could hang around town. John and Amelia wanted to stay at the table and chat. I got to the dock, but then returned to the restaurant to retrieve my sunglasses. As I returned, Amelia was smiling at something John had said, and I was so pleased that she was enjoying this private time with her father.

As I got closer, I saw John's hands under the table, pouring something

into his cola from the flask bottle. I just couldn't believe what I was seeing. I grabbed Amelia and left for the boat. John called his old AA sponsor back in California and came back to the boat around midnight. It was
a hard time. The next day he would have to tell the kids all about his history with alcohol and start over. So he did that. "The thing about Dad,"
he began. He spared no detail.

"If *alk-ee-hall* tastes so bad, why do you drink it, anyway?" little Jack
asked at the conclusion. Amelia was hurt. She felt she had been lied to all
these years. She wanted to know how she got so lucky to have an alcoholic father. He promised her he would never take another drink. Ben
was silent, withdrawn. Little Camille was aware something bad was happening, but was anxious to get on with it and back to something more
fun. I did not speak. I was hiding my red eyes behind my sunglasses. The
AA meetings on the island were a mixture of old harbor rummies and
yachtsmen. He went.

All that January in 2004, John worked on the new bimini and went to
meetings, his local sponsor picking him up in a runabout. There were
some continuing problems with one of the engines.

The children seemed content. There was a school on Water Island
that they could attend three days a week—even Camille could go. This
sort of thing would always be in addition to the correspondence schoolwork. Amelia and Ben became certified scuba divers. Ben began spear-
fishing with new friends. Jack even acquired a baby land tortoise, Speedy.

Alcohol is a tough bird. On Jack's eighth birthday, we rented a car and
drove over to Red Hook for windsurfing lessons. Afterward, while I was
ordering Chinese takeout, John went to "find a paper" at the news store
across the street.

I came out of the Chinese restaurant and found Amelia crying hyster-
ically. As I tried to calm her, she explained that she had run across to
the store to buy some gum. She saw John at the checkout counter with
two miniature bottles of vodka. John then appeared, his eyes darting
anxiously.

"How could you do this?" I demanded.

"I didn't *do* anything," he insisted.

Amelia knew he was lying. So did I. So did he.

He walked over to a trash can and threw the bottles away.

An uneasiness settled over the family. We were back at sea in early February, leaving the Virgin Islands to explore the more southern islands. We stopped to spend a day in Saba, a dark, volcanic fang rising sharply from the water. John was commanding his crew, but he did so now as a damaged leader. The rocky monolith ahead, now almost in the dark as we neared, seemed somehow right. It wasn't beautiful, but it was real. Some of the world's finest diving is in its waters, where lava tubes are nurseries for a profusion of tropical life. But the moorings around it were churning with wild surf. It was soon dark night. This would be a hard passage.

Ben bravely rode the lurching starboard bow like a surfboard. He held a strong flashlight, searching the sea for a mooring buoy. He found it in his light and held the narrow beam on it, though the deck tossed him up and down. The breaking waves were terribly close to the buoy and to the cliffs of this dark castle of an island.

"What does that mooring look like to you, son?" John yelled forward.

"Kinda grungy, Dad," was the reply, meaning it might not be secure enough for our big boat.

Amelia peered out into the salt spray from under the bimini and watched Ben and her father maneuver ever closer to the buoy. I came out and gave John a hard time for taking so long—I wanted off this ride. John yelled to me over the surf that the mooring was too close. If it was not strong enough for this sea, and if it broke loose, we would have no time to get the engines running to get away from the surf and the rock.

I said something brilliant like, "Just show some guts and let's get it done," and I went below.

Amelia, whose seafaring sensibilities had matured, looked at John and mouthed "No." She knew her Dad and Ben were right about this place. It was spooky and wrong. John hit the engine and turned the boat toward the open sea. I came up and was shouting at him. At the time, I just didn't get the danger of the situation and was not really in the mood for it. Without meaning to, I gave Ben and Amelia an important moment with their father—a moment they needed very much: They were starting to trust him again. We headed to Saint Kitts through the night. Ben and Amelia set the genoa as the night smoothed beautifully under a southerly breeze. We were moving. Amelia watched the stars for a while and then came below for some sleep; Ben sailed with his Dad through most of the night.

In Saint Kitts, we explored a rain forest full of monkeys. Later, Amelia was sure she spotted Prince William in a shop with his bodyguards; the huge *Queen Mary 2* was anchored in port on her first sail through the Caribbean. Ben went scuba diving, Jack fished from the dock, and Camille and I relaxed on the boat while John found a mechanic to repair the engine. It griped him to call in someone for that, as he considered himself a good tool man. But these engines were big and complicated and beyond his experience. When they were purring again, we hoisted the sails and, within a few hours, were gliding into Nevis.

———

On the beach, Ben was starting to notice girls more and more, and there were a lot to see on these beaches and at the lavish Four Seasons resort swimming pools. He still had a hard time striking up a conversation. His little brother was more sure of his biological pursuits: Jack scoured the ocean bottom off the fancy beach for creatures he could capture in his peanut butter jar.

Watching over him, parked in the sand with Camille, Amelia sunned herself and read to her baby sister from storybooks. As for me, I had a firm grip on the fact that this was a resort: I had a massage in a cabana under the coconut palms.

Near the pool, John stretched back on a plush chaise longue, staring out at the *Emerald Jane,* which looked fine, holding her own among the other boats. The kids slowly collected around him. Amelia asked him if he would go up to the thatched outdoor cocktail bar and get them all virgin piña coladas, her new favorite beverage. At the bar, the dreadlocked bartender poured to the reggae beat of a piped-in Bob Marley—"No Woman, No Cry." In this moment, John slipped. He saw the magic bottles lined up and told the bartender to add a screwdriver to the tab. Doubles were on sale. Fine. He had one. Drank it right down. And another.

"Get your things," I ordered the children as I returned from my massage and could see that John was not just being talkative to the beach attendant—he was a blur.

Back on board, Amelia went into her cabin crying. Ben was stoic but clearly disgusted. Jack plopped down on a cockpit bench to study John and me like sea specimens. He was interested in what we might do. He liked a good show. Camille was confused, on the verge of tears, but Jack kept her busy with the crab in his jar.

We had at it. It ended as such things usually do. John said, "Well, the hell with it. The hell with everybody."

He staggered through the cockpit toward our cabin. I could hear him slamming drawers down there. Jack slipped quietly into the salon and went to the chart table where the boat's papers were kept. Jack quickly found his father's passport and hid it away in his own pocket. Then he went back to his 50-yard-line seat in the cockpit.

When John reappeared topside, he had a small duffel, half unzipped, with a polo shirt hanging out.

"I'm leaving," he proclaimed. "Screw you, Jean. And screw this trip." He stepped onto the stairs and fumbled to untie the dinghy. I tried to stop him but he almost sent me into the water.

That's when I pushed his shoulder and he tumbled into the water.

He struggled back aboard and went dripping below, all four kids now staring at him and at me.

Jack figured that was all there was to see, and he went on to another project.

I just sat there in the late afternoon sun, gazing at this beautiful green island where the clouds roll across the shoulders of the mountain. Camille crept over and curled into my embrace; I could feel her tears wetting my lap.

In a little while, I went into the hotel and bought plane tickets to the States for myself and the kids. Captain John could jolly well fend for himself. The first available flight wasn't for a few days.

That night everyone on board was a zombie. Ben cooked the hamburgers on the grill on the stern, then he flipped them into the water. Amelia asked me, in such a dead way, why her father had lied to her.

I made the usual speech that is made at such times: "Daddy is an alcoholic and doesn't mean to lie. He really thought he wasn't going to drink again when he made that promise. He really loves you," blah, blah blah.

The next morning, John hopped out of bed as if nothing had happened. He made his patented chocolate-chip pancakes and started cleaning the boat like a madman. Jack informed him that he was keeping his passport for a while.

Alone in bed for a second night, I realized I didn't really want to live without him. He was trouble, but life is trouble. The question always has to be, *is he worth it?* John was.

From there, we headed away from that Jimmy Buffett world and toward islands more of our own.

Leaving any island had many of the same routines: Ben and Amelia will bring the dinghy alongside with supplies from a village grocery store. The little ones will march the grocery bags across the deck, through the salon, and down into the galley, where I will put everything away if I can somehow find room, which somehow happens. Amelia will join me and we'll talk about stuff.

John and Ben will swing the arched, stainless davits into place to hoist the dinghy up snug on the stern. Ben then yells for Amelia to come up from below to help him hoist the anchor—a messy job. The chain and anchor have to be cleaned with a brush and laid out, the chain in rows, in its locker. Someone has to get down into that dirty chain locker and do it. Ben and Amelia no longer complain about it; it's just something that needs doing.

Leaving Nevis, John started the two diesel engines and nudged the boat forward as the anchor came up. When he heard "anchor's up," he turned the boat toward the sea.

This was, as always, my cue to come aft and take the wheel from John as he and Amelia and Ben prepare to hoist the mainsail like a great flag. It is heavy work, but they have grown strong. Ben shackles the sail to the strong rope, called the halyard, which goes up to the pulley at the top of the mast. The "lazy jacks" are freed. They are lines running from the top of the mast down to the big horizontal boom. You tighten them when you are lowering the sail so it will stack in pleats on the boom. But you have to loosen those lazy-jack lines when you are hauling the sail up, because they will get in the way of the sail filling with wind. A few thousand miles ago, John would shout for the lazy jacks to be freed, but now all that just happened.

I carefully gauge the wind's direction, ready to turn the wheel to keep *Emerald Jane's* bows pointed into the wind so the sail will stay slack until it was all the way up and we were ready.

At this point, John will usually go into his pirate mode: "Look away, me lads, and hoist the sail! Let fly the Jolly Roger! Look away, me lads—I said, hoist the sail and be bloody buccaneers!" A few thousand miles ago, Ben and Amelia would tell him to stop it—that it was embarrassing when boats with other teens were in the harbor. Now they smile at their father. Even his late embarrassments will not stop his hoist traditions.

Then John pulls hard on the halyard as the great sail, linked along the mast, begins to rise into the sky. He will soon wrap the halyard three times around a giant hourglass-shaped winch on the base of the mast. The big handle on the winch turns as John, Ben, and Amelia take turns applying their full weight. The sail rises higher and higher—eight stories of heavy fabric. By tradition, Amelia will crank the very last and hardest fifteen feet. In a heavy wind, the sail might be "reefed," or lowered partway.

John will then free the line that holds the big horizontal boom in suspension over the deck, as the sail will now keep the boom well aloft.

The three of them will scramble back to me in the cockpit. John will kill the engines and one of the two of us will turn the big wheel to let the wind catch the sail and the boat take her course. The wind is usually coming off from the side or the aft, but a sailboat can cut into the wind—not directly but at about a 45-degree angle—because the curve of the sail acts like an airplane wing: the low pressure on the bulging side pulls the boat along while the wind pushes from the inside. There are enough forces at work over and under the boat to confuse nature a bit and allow the boat to speed against the wind. For the sailor, there is some satisfaction in modestly cheating nature in this way, though it is a trick mastered better by any gliding seagull.

Amelia and Ben will check the portholes and the skylight hatches along the deck; forgetting to snap them shut could mean wet bedsheets that night for somebody.

The huge mainsail will suddenly fill with breeze with a snap-bang. Ben will lash the big boom to a cleat, lest an errant gust send it swinging toward us.

There is the smaller sail up at the bow, the genoa jib, and we have a smaller crew for that one. It is mostly Jack's job to unfurl and set the genoa. His freckled face is intently serious for this task. "Set it to starboard, Dad?" He will guess it right, of course.

He carries forward with him a big handle for the genoa's winch, and will soon have the sail unfurled and billowing ahead of us, pulling us over the waves an extra knot or two faster.

"Way to go!" John will yell to him over the bouncing boom and splash of the boat.

Jack will wave back.

There will soon be breakfast smells wafting up from the galley. John will check the GPS and his charts. Camille and Jack will set the cockpit table. Jack will soon be banging his spoon and fork on the cockpit table to demand service for a hungry mate.

The adventures of each moment were all the medicine John needed— life was just beautiful. Just the same, at my suggestion, he met in Saint Lucia with an East Indian woman who used transcendental meditation to help people with addictions. John is averse to that kind of woo-woo, but he went back for a second session and a third, looking for inner experiences to keep him whole and happy.

WORKING WITH THE WAVES

"**B**ig one coming." The sound of the wave alerted me to its size before I saw the house-high comber roaring onto the reef. We braced for the impact as the wave struck: the raft, although still tethered to the deck, wildly bucked the ride and nearly capsized; the mast rolled again on John's leg—he was screaming as he went under the water. Ben used this wave motion to wedge things under the mast, preparing to make one great last effort to move it. Then again: "Another big one!" This looked like the end—huge new waves to finish the job.

———

In Alameda, California, Coast Guard Petty Officer Kevin Denicker was trying to make sense of the ambiguous signals coming from the grail in Jack's embrace. After contacting family members who knew our sailing schedule, Denicker narrowed the prospective search area from two million square miles down to a Texas-sized quarter-million. But without a stronger signal and better information from our beacon, he couldn't really begin a search. Maritime officers manning satellite ground

stations in Australia, New Zealand, and France waited with him for better informa-
tion that everyone knew might never come.

———

John's mind was adrift—his consciousness battered by shock and toxic buildups in his remaining blood. His thoughts were fracturing into a kaleidoscope of waking nightmares.

In his thoughts he stood at the wheel again. We were off the Guajira Peninsula at night, trying to outrun Colombian pirates. He was hunched over the engine throttles, squeezing out the last available power to escape a long string of pirate boats coming ever closer. His hands thrashed about, gripping the familiar controls and the lines of the rigging. He imagined the lines and sails tangled over the deck, and himself shrouded under them, and then under the water, trapped beneath the stern—his lungs filling with the warm sea.

"Big one!" he heard time and again in the distance.

Ben and I struggled for three hours to free him. The mast occasionally lifted a few inches and then slammed down again. John heard our muffled curses as our hands slipped on the wet metal.

"Big one!" How this phrase marked time through the long night! John, in moments of clarity, marveled that his family was working together as never before.

The crashing sea was gradually twisting the wreckage of our home around. The twin bows now faced the open sea. The stern, with its little ladders on each aft, was now banging on the highest growths of coral. The decks, which had been riding atop the splinters of wreckage, now themselves were split and shattered.

Ben had been noticing a particular coral shelf. He never saw the water wash high over it. It might be a place to go when the boat collapsed beneath us, which could happen at any moment.

From the exposed tops of the coral, we could see that the tide was going out. There would be a great flow of water from the inland lagoon back into the sea. There was a good chance that it would sweep us out to sea. John would go down quickly with the mast. It was time to do something.

Watching Ben prepare for our next effort to move the mast, it occurred to me that my legs were far stronger than my arms. I knew this from the weights I could lift at my gym back home.

As the next huge wave broke, I was on my back pushing up and out against the mast. Ben was pulling with his strong arms. John felt the familiar elevator lift of the boat as the swell built under us. The wave crested above us, submerging John. But he sensed that something had changed. He forced himself upright on his elbows and pushed his body back. The mast and the sharp-edged line spreader slammed back down.

He was free.

[8]

GROWING UP AT SEA

"**D**ad, are you okay?" Amelia almost pounced on him. His teeth were chattering horribly, but he managed an affirmative sound.

Ben knelt beside them, clutching a coil of thin line and some tools.

"Gotta do the tourniquet again, Dad. It's gonna hurt."

He turned to his sister. "Amelia, help with this line, but don't look."

"Just do it. Hurry," she replied. It was clear that the mast itself had been part of the tourniquet and John was in danger of losing the last of his blood in the next few minutes.

Amelia did look: The skin was off the shin; an exposed muscle was swollen like a red balloon; the shattered bones were a visible wreck; the lower leg hung from a few shreds of skin and tendon. Blood, black blood, was spurting out with his every heartbeat. She decided to be strong like Ben.

They bent to their task, knees awash in their father's blood. Ben wound the new knot tighter and tighter. It was utterly dark on deck except for Ben's green glow stick. I watched as they worked on their father with such moral strength.

———

They had matured quickly, really starting with John's bout with alcohol. After that crisis, smaller problems just were easier to see in perspective and the sibling warfare faded away, though by fits and starts.

In the months after we sailed from Nevis and our problems there, we found ourselves far from the tourist resorts, exploring the lesser-traveled islands on our own. We anchored in isolated bays surrounded by noisy jungles and dramatic volcanic ridges.

The kids fell into a cheerful rhythm with their chores and schoolwork. Sailing in rough weather had always made reading and writing almost impossible, but now everything was easier. We were finding the calm anchorages we needed for family and private time. They were so filled with beauty and activity that John—and you really cannot overstimulate this man—was just a brilliant dad and husband.

A "school day" began at 7:00 a.m. with a family breakfast, then everybody cleaned their rooms. We took turns cooking and rotated cleaning up the kitchen: The same person washed all the dishes for all three meals for one week. That way there were fewer "No, it's your turn" arguments.

Schoolwork itself began at 8:00 a.m., when I returned from a morning run on the beach. Ben worked at the desk in his room; Amelia on her bed and sometimes at her desk; Jack studied at the dining table, while Camille used the cockpit table outside or the salon's chart table. They took fifteen-minute breaks at 9:30 and 11:00, and were finished by noon.

Ben's curriculum was the most difficult, so John tutored him in Spanish, biology, chemistry, geometry, and Algebra II. These were tough courses, but Ben stayed ahead of his friends back home. I worked with him on English, World Cultures, and U.S. History. He was responsible for all the work, but we made sure the packets were complete before we sent them. When we were in a port with an Internet café, Ben would take his tests online.

Amelia's middle-school curriculum included pre-Algebra, Algebra, History, English, and Science. John helped with the math, and I tutored on the rest. Amelia had a weekly assignment list, but no tests. We mailed the completed material once a month to the San Diego homeschooling program.

Jack's second- and third-grade material was almost entirely done in workbooks, which we also mailed monthly to California. While the older kids studied well on their own, Jack was easily distracted and needed the most help. I had to work one-on-one with him for a few hours a day.

My real concern was that they would become very bored without the organized hobbies and sports that had once filled their afternoons. But after studying all morning they never tired of snorkeling, scuba diving, or exploring some quiet island beach. They just didn't seem to miss organized sports or competition. Ben and Amelia became enthusiastic about visiting the old colonial waterfronts and forts, even the museums.

Arriving at a new island became a big event for them: They collected samples of local currency in bills and coins, insisted that their passports be clearly stamped, and then explored all the sites.

John, who received his passport back from Jack in a private ceremony I knew meant much to John, claimed he hadn't even thought about alcohol since leaving the resort islands. The rift of anger between the two of us was healing; we were slipping away to secluded beaches when we could, and that made all the difference. We were rediscovering the energies that had first brought us together.

I tried to loosen the knots of anger that had really been so much a part of me during the trip.

The mornings, especially, were my time.

When I have my my coffee at the cockpit table, with everyone else still asleep below, the quiet of the morning in an anchorage is itself a calming meditation. The silence is not absolute: I can hear the crusty ceramic edge of my coffee mug every time I set it on the table; there is the sound of my drinking it, breathing the steam. The sea around me laps with little slaps and splashes along the hulls, and there is the clank and chime of lines and pulleys nearby and high on the mast, playing triangle to the sea's quiet passages. The distant shouts and laughter of someone else's kid's— native kids, probably—travel so far you have to squint to see them playing in the surf a long way down the beach, chasing around on black, shiny pedestals of coral. The sunrise, made gauzy by the morning fog, brings with it little breezes that flap the limpid canvas of the bimini and the folded sails. Distant jungle birds, noticeable mostly when they stop for a moment, pressurize the atmosphere like crickets and cicadas on an American summer evening.

Nothing smells like the sea, of course. Nothing so refreshes your nostrils and your life. If there is a pier or wharf or jetty nearby, then there is an honest, fishy smell that is friendly and agreeable. The scent of diesel smoke may drift across from somewhere; it is a sea smell, too, and mixes nicely with the sounds—the ding and flap and little splashes. Seagulls are royalty; no sound or sight does more to stamp the moment officially as nautical and free.

I would try to let all thoughts slip away with the little splashes against the ship, and let all worries rise up like a vapor through the lines of the mast—up and away. Here we are. My family is waking up. We are here in the beauty of the world. Let me be as happy, Lord, as I ought to be.

The cool salt air; some distant lump in the sea—what is it?—maybe a cross-blown wave or a dolphin. You stand and stare out at it for a long while, sipping, breathing deeply, matching your body to the slow roll of the deck. Stretching. Thinking about taking a beach run. How strange to be alive. How very, very long the world has been here without us. How very long it will be here after us. How strange to be so privileged among creatures to have this special consciousness of it, though not for long, not for long. *How strange to not be here forever.* The gulls call back and forth as they move in casual formation between the ship and the distant palms; pelicans dive for their morning feast. How very strange it all sometimes seems.

On March 31, 2004, we tied up in a marina on the sheltered west coast of Grenada, the southernmost island of the Lesser Antilles. If Bermuda, the Virgin Islands, and the many other islands that crumble from Florida past Cuba and Haiti can be thought of as a grand spine curving leeward through the hurricane latitudes—toward the top of South America and almost touching it—we were moored there at the last bone of it, so very far from home. John stood in the cockpit watching through binoculars as Steffan Van Zwam brought *Fruity Fruits* into the wind and dropped anchor out in True Blue Bay. We had not seen the Van Zwams since Bermuda, and Steffan had an important reason for catching up with us.

"Carolyne and I would like *Emerald Jane* to cruise with us to Panama and then into the Pacific," he grandly announced. "It would be safer for us to sail west together—safer from pirates and all that."

Nicely rehearsed. He had talked to John about this over the radio. John was, naturally, all for it. But the new course would mean many more months at sea, and the kids were just starting to get excited about going home to their old life. Maybe I was, too.

We had only just arrived in Grenada when our diesel-powered generator clanked to a permanent halt and sent a question mark of greasy smoke into the blue sky. We would have to replace the unit soon, as it powered the appliances and the water-desalting system that provided our fresh water. In the meantime, we would have to fill our water tanks and ration water when away from the dock.

We could get a new generator in Grenada but it would take six weeks and would be more costly than if we went back to the Virgin Islands, now far to our north, or in Panama, over a thousand miles west across the northern brow of South America. If we went to Panama, skirting along dangerous pirate waters, we would be committed to go through the canal into the Pacific, as the spring and summer trade winds make it nearly impossible for a sailboat to go from Panama eastward back to the Virgins. So the black, smoky question mark was whether we should retrace our journey or strike out for the Pacific. The Pacific loomed in our minds as the serious ocean; the Caribbean, by comparison, was a yacht harbor.

Amelia was becoming an interested and competent navigator, and she understood the question very well. She wanted to go home, but she had decided to not make a dramatic scene—she knew she could leave that to her big brother. But Ben, helping John repair the radio as John raised the subject, seemed resigned to the Pacific journey. Not happy, but resigned.

Getting ready for Amelia's thirteenth birthday party, John and I talked privately. I wanted to know if he would do better closer to his San Diego AA pals. I told him I couldn't handle another fall from the wagon on this trip—that was the deciding issue for me. He said hadn't had a drink since Nevis, but he was only making promises one day at a time. He said the Pacific journey would be the crowning event of his life and of all his dreams.

The next day, we had tea with Steffan and Carolyne on their boat in True Blue Bay. Steffan unrolled several large charts and showed the route to Panama, by way of Bonaire, Curaçao, and Aruba. John saw my continuing hesitation and said we would talk it over and get back to them.

The next morning I went for an early run above True Blue Bay. Carolyne loved to run in the mornings, too, and we would often meet up whenever we were on the same island. We would talk a little during the run and a little more after. We would make plans. Sometimes she would take all the kids over on their boat so John and I could have some time alone. Sometimes we did that for them. "It's so hard being so bloody quiet," she had complained about trying to have intimate moments when others were on board.

I ran alone this morning to think. Grenada is a beautiful place; the people are friendly and will smile and wave as you run by their little houses. These people rose up to oppose a dictator back in the eighties, but after a series of coups they ended up with American troops in their land. However they might feel about all that, they are kind to Americans.

The Van Z's boat was so beautiful to see, anchored far below in True Blue Bay; ours was docked around a spit of land in the marina. I was moving along in the crisp air, the dirt of an old residential street crunching as I ran. Steffan is a great guy. He has been so long at this stuff that he easily repairs his own boat, while we are forever hiring expensive mechanics and waiting for them to arrive and to finish. I know how frustrating this is for John. He sailed a great deal as a young man, but he was still new to this boat and to some of its complex mechanical systems. It is not fair to compare. The palms and the thick jungles of a morning run, the sound of birds and—what is that?—monkeys maybe. There is no young Rasta man on a bicycle behind me this time, like there was on Union Island in the Tobago Cays. He rode behind me, not the least bit scary, just to visit and tell me I had shaped my body very well with my exercise. I took him as a would-be personal trainer and not as a would-be romancer, and we had a good run and ride. No, the thing about Steffan is that he is so oddly perfect—a handsome diamond cutter, for heaven's sake, like the Lord put him in our company for John to compare himself to, and quite unfairly.

John is mechanic enough, and has had business success enough. I mean, here we are. Look down at the beach and the beautiful colors of the water. John made this happen. Of course, I made it happen, too. I suppose Carolyne helps Steffan. There are little stores and open-air restaurants along the roads. People are getting them ready for the day.

I was thinking that I really wanted to see Aruba and Bonaire. Bonaire is supposed to have the best scuba diving in the world. Those islands are to the west of Grenada, and if you go there in this season, it's very hard to get back to the Virgin Islands because of the strong westerly winds, as I mentioned. You have to put your boat somewhere safe before hurricane season starts. Many people go back to the United States with their boats, starting about now. And if we went all the way to Panama, of course, it would be impossible. We would have to go all the way through the canal. Even then we would have some options: We could go up the Pacific to California, or, if things really fell apart with John, the kids and I could just get on a plane in Panama and that would be it. We would need a place to stay in California, since the house was occupied. No good options there. It is so hard when you are watching someone's every move all the time, wondering and not trusting. Is a slurred word just a trip of the tongue, or a trip-up? Should the trash be examined? Should he go to stores alone? It is wearying and maddening. And to see the same fear and uncertainty in the kids' eyes, wondering if Dad is in too good a mood—does it mean something bad? Do we have to worry every time he tells a joke? I had the satisfaction of believing that he would never drink on the boat at sea. And yet he stayed dry for, what? Twelve years or more. If he only slips up every twelve years, what do I think about that?

And pirates? What is a mother to think about all that? The worst of the stories were not shared with me, owing to John's confidence in the speed of *Emerald Jane.* I knew that sailors always needed to be careful in these waters—that has always been the case. But you see harbors filled with fancy boats and you can put all the danger out of your mind, like when you step inside an airplane. And I wasn't going to let us get into ports or areas that were too scary. I always had faith in my cautious nature.

Grenada is one of the Spice Islands. Cinnamon, ginger, cloves, a fifth of the world's nutmeg. It does not smell of spices when you run, except the citrus here and there, but it smells fresh and cool. A nutmeg is on the flag of Grenada. My thoughts turned to California as I ran. John built nice entry-level houses and they sold well even though the market was still pretty bad. I did all the books for the company, oversaw the marketing, worked with the architects and decorators, got pregnant with Jack. I had to start working in the same office with John. It became difficult working together and being with each other all the time. My pregnancy hormones didn't help. The thing is, if John is not working and I am, I get upset. He is a controlling personality, and so am I. The several employees didn't like my giving orders and they would tell John, "Jean is running the show; you need to be running the show." I liked to get things done and John liked to talk. That's okay because talking is where the deals are made. He was big picture; I was details. That's a good team, but the differences created huge strains on our relationship.

So. Same thing. I go out for a run in the morning after writing in my journal and answering e-mails, taking care of business. I come back and he will be relaxing in the cockpit, drinking coffee. He got up before I left so I know he has been there an hour or so, drinking coffee. I will then eat breakfast and start the kids on their schoolwork and do some cleaning while the kids are working and calling me to help with problems or questions. Meanwhile, John will maybe be finishing his morning swim. There is always something to fix on a boat. "Shouldn't you be..." Like that.

Nutmegs. Spice Islands. Who's the nut? I am. I think about it as I run—what a place we are in. John gets it. I'm worrying and not enjoying the moment. I haven't been able to settle down into this trip—can't live in the moment, always thinking about what comes next. Maybe he has forced me to be this way. As soon as I explore an island or area, I'm ready to be off to the next one. John will want to stay and enjoy the area. After all, it's a paradise of total sensory overload, which is what he always needs and what everything here really is. I have a powerful restlessness that John doesn't share. We were anchored in the Tobago Cays—so gorgeous—the two younger ones and John could have spent a week there. I wanted to leave after just a few days—my mind is always racing to the next place. I don't know if it is a sickness or what. I see the rusty cannons of the old fort overlooking the sea—I didn't mean to come this far.

This was John's dream but, God, I love to travel, too, any kind of travel, and if I had to go by boat, that was fine. Every time we went down to the marina in San Diego, maybe for an afternoon charter during the years when we didn't own a boat, I so missed being a part of that world. I had a longing for the community showers, the sitting on decks at sunrise with coffee and at sunset with wine. The smell of fresh varnish. Everything we did financially was geared toward this goal. Whenever I would spend too much on something frivolous, I would give myself a stern lecture. If John was overbudget on a project, I would remind him of the dream, and that if he didn't negotiate or cut back on something, the trip couldn't happen. It all clicked together—his genius for the present and my genius for the future, or something like that. And if he had some character flaws, well, you need to see people's flaws in perspective with their good qualities—no one is just the one thing; everybody is complex; everything is a compromise. A marriage is that. A friendship is even that.

We had come so far.

I was out of breath.

When I came back from my run, John was enjoying his coffee. Gave me a big, stupid smile as I caught my breath on deck. I gave him a little present from the marina store: nautical maps to Panama.

There would be hard moments yet ahead, but something about the family had changed deeply, and for the better, ever since the drinking crisis. I could see John a little more clearly, and I could see clearly now what Ben and Amelia would be like as adults.

———

And on the reef now—oh, I hate to go back—there they were, it seemed, all grown.

"Mom, we gotta get him warm somehow," Ben said.

Amelia, Ben, and I carefully picked up John, supporting his dangling lower leg as best we could, and carried him into the life raft beside the boat. In terrible pain from this move, he settled in between Jack and Camille, who cuddled to warm him. The red light of the rescue beacon was not red enough to make John's face look other than the ashen mask it had become.

The deck was bucking violently and the raft was suddenly being pulled back to the boat by the tangle of lines.

"Everyone out," I said. Camille and Jack jumped out as it bent over the edge. I pulled John out, his ghastly leg dangling. In a tug-of-war with the sea, I zipped the raft's canopy to protect Speedy and the food and water supplies inside.

Emerald Jane's hulls buckled wildly. With a great crack, our starboard side broke in two and jackknifed against itself, snaring the life raft in a great vise and binding it in a net of rigging, half in the water between the hull pieces. If the boat went down now, the raft would go down in its embrace.

Jack was crying—not for himself and not for his father, but for Speedy. This was a crisis he knew how to process; everything else was too big for now.

"He's safer in there," I explained. "There's too much happening out here, Jack. You might drop him. You need to hold the beacon." That was good enough. He nodded.

Ben and Amelia shepherded Jack and Camille aft to the relative shelter of the cockpit, still riding above the breaking hulls. Ben returned with a short saw blade from the tool locker.

"God, Ben, no," I said when I saw it in his hand. I was sitting on the deck next to John

"It's to free the lifeboat, Mom."

Before he could cut the tangled lines, another monster wave hit and sent the raft farther into the churning water. The broken section of the starboard hull still gripped it against the boat. The raft's bright red canopy was tearing.

Ben and I managed to carry John aft. The starboard side, where we had been stuck, was coming apart rapidly, so we moved John and the kids to port stern. Amelia guided us over the jumbled decks by the faint light of a glow stick; John could not afford to have us trip and fall.

Camille sat up at the wheel, staring out into the dark sea. I had never seen her so sad and still. Five years old. Soaking wet and so cold. How did we allow this to happen to her?

Camille had come into our lives as the unexpected fourth child. Like Jack, she came easily. Ben had been a tough delivery, and Amelia a bit rough. But Jack was easy and Camille just sort of floated out, glowing with such joy.

It happened after John and I stopped working together in the same office. We did that to save our marriage. But we could do something: We decided to take the vacant lot we owned next to our home and build a real house for us, selling our old one when we were finished. We were building other houses at the time, so we could get materials and services at tract pricing. John ran the grading operations and I managed the construction of the home. The fact that we lived next door made it easy to go back and forth and oversee the contractors. I worked with the architect and designer.

When the house was framed, dry-walled, and plastered, I was walking around in it and I started feeling dizzy and confused. I was standing in the master bedroom wondering what was going on. Then it hit me: I was pregnant. A fourth and very unplanned baby. John was forty-seven and I was forty. Dear God.

I worried how this would affect our plans for the house and for the dream of sailing, since I had been sure we were finally finished with diapers and cribs. I went through a week or two of shock. I had given all the baby stuff away. The new house didn't really accommodate a fourth child, and I didn't have time for the three children I already had.

Friends told me that a surprise child is the best. She was, indeed, magical from the very first.

Ben, who had grown used to fighting with Jack and Amelia, took her instantly under his wing. Jack teased her mercilessly, but there was great love in it—she was a beautiful creature to be around. Her early teachers always just looked at me during conferences as if to ask, "Where did this child come from?" She was always one of their favorites, and in an almost transformational way. She was the bright Japanese lantern we didn't even know our garden needed.

Sitting by the great steel wheel, Camille turned and looked me in the eye and said in her shivering voice, "Mommy, if I go to heaven, I want you to come with me. And I want Daddy to stop hurting."

I wrapped my arms around her for a long while. I said I would always be with her. I hoped that was so. She returned to her distant gaze and I let her be.

A great wave ripped apart the canvas bimini and sent its steel struts flying. One came at Camille like a spear, barely missing her. I moved her to the port stern. Immediately after that, a heavy winch handle flew, grazing Jack's head—it could easily have killed him. The boat was coming apart fast and we needed to get off.

The ripping sounds of the boat were constant and vicious; the sound never let up. The ruined cockpit was now continuously swept by breaking waves. The port-side deck became our remaining few square feet of dark refuge.

Ben and I struggled to shelter John from the chill spray with our bodies. Amelia wrapped Jack and Camille in her arms, with the cold waves crashing against her back. I held John's hands, but he could not return the squeeze. He was rapidly fading.

When the waves let up for a moment, Amelia spotted a blue bungee cord swirling in the water of the cockpit. Young Jack crawled to fetch it. She made an additional tourniquet over the old one, as blood had continued to flow from the hideous wound. It was grisly work. She started hesitantly with her face distorted by the horror of it, but she settled into the

project, knowing that John was feeling the incredible pain of it but determined to stop the blood once and for all. Her face became serious, ma-
turely professional. She gave her father a running account of what she
was doing and what she was seeing. She could have done anything necessary in that moment of growing up. She then got up and tore a piece of
canvas from the tattered bimini to cover him.

"Look!" Jack shouted, pointing eastward.

A glow on the horizon—maybe the lights of a big ship. Ben scrambled for the flares and fired one high into the night.

[9]

SHOOTING THE MOON

"They've found us," I cried, ecstatic.

Ben fired another flare—so beautiful, so full of ruby-bright promise. The light on the horizon swelled oddly. It was the moon, passing through the thin gap between the horizon and the cover of distant clouds. Total darkness again. For a long time we crouched together on the stern, keeping John as warm as we could, hoping that the red-glowing beacon was doing something. Amelia asked me what the plan was now. I said we didn't have a plan except to stay alive and pray. So we prayed together. The moon came out of the clouds from time to time; otherwise we had only the green of some glow sticks. Camille and Jack fell asleep off and on in Amelia's arms, and kept waking up to the same nightmare. Ben and I sandwiched John upright between us, sitting on the stern.

The *Emerald Jane* had swung around with its broken bows now facing the sea; a floating flap of our wrecked ship mercifully raised up with each incoming wave to protect us where we huddled. Again and again, big waves came close, began to break over us, and then this hand rose up to shield us. The same rotation of the boat that had improved the beacon's signal now gave us a bit of shelter from the cold sea.

John was on the edge of consciousness. He was working hard to become one with the pain, to accept it. The lurch of the boat would make him cry out a little. Then he would worry and mumble about something that wasn't there: a dragging anchor, pirates off the port side.

He was reliving the voyage in his imagination. We had been through so many moments that seemed now like dreams.

I had not taken too seriously John and Steffan's conversations and preparations regarding pirates as we left Grenada for the Panama Canal—boys playing, was what it sounded like. John was concerned that we were unarmed, though he took some comfort in knowing we had a flare gun that was probably as good as a shotgun.

There were many stories floating around the Caribbean harbors—stories people don't talk about unless you bring up the subject, as the newspapers and governments don't like reporting such things—bad for business. But just ask around: Oh, yes, a married couple brutalized and the husband killed over off that island; a sailboat chased down by a speedboat of armed men in February. The yacht captain was shot dead on deck after the pirates stripped the boat of its electronics and other valuables. South of the island of Bonaire, which was on our route, innocent hands and arms and backs had been sliced to the *bone* by machete-wielding pirates boarding a boat. A European couple, anchored in a quiet bay, woke to find pirates tying the wife's hands. The husband was badly cut when he tried to defend her. These were recent attacks.

Steffan and Carolyne had one story firsthand: A small French yacht, *Myriad*, belonged to their friend.

"Pirates slunk up alongside *Myriad* after dark in one of those little *peñero* boats," Steffan told us over lunch in Grenada. "In the blink of an eye, Robert saw a chap with a shotgun climbing on deck, so he ran to his cabin and managed to lock the door. While he was loading his flare gun, the pirate smashed the shotgun barrel through the cabin door and fired. Robert ducked and was just missed by the blast. He fired back with his flare gun—the flare blasted out the door toward the invaders, wounding one of them, and the buggers ran! Carolyne helped Robert write his police report, so we got the whole story."

We began to think we had gotten off easily several islands earlier when we suffered our own close encounter. It was on Saint Vincent, one of the islands where *Pirates of the Caribbean* had been filmed—some of the movie sets were still visible.

We had anchored in a bay under the steep green slopes of La Soufrière volcano. There was a small village on the shore, and only one other boat moored in the bay—an abandoned ship that looked a bit spooky.

Amelia and I jumped into the dinghy and headed into the village to shop for fresh mangos and bananas, and maybe to find a guide to take us on a hike up the volcano the following day. As we tied up and locked the dinghy on the dock, we were surrounded by the foulest-looking people, toothless and dirty, zombielike as they followed us. No wonder *Pirates of the Caribbean* was shot here, I was thinking: A camera pointed in any direction would do for the casting. A layer of marijuana smoke filled the village. We bought our fruit and pushed back through the men to our dinghy, still there, and left for the safety of the boat. But while we were ashore, a group of even ghastlier-looking men had paddled old dugout canoes up to the *Emerald Jane,* where Ben and Jack were snorkeling off the stern. The men surrounded the boys and offered to watch the boat—keep it safe, you know, for a donation, please. They paddled into a closer circle. On a tattered windsurfing board, one man clung to the stern, offering a collection of bruised fruit at an exorbitant price. John came up on deck and saw the situation and sent the men away.

"They're crazy on shore, too," I reported. Amelia was in shock as she confirmed my assessment.

We gazed landward with our binoculars: Ragged men stood everywhere in the shade of the shacks, staring back at us. Their look of hunger and desperation was both heartbreaking and frightening. We Americans do not often see the big part of the world that lives on less than a dollar a day.

No one had threatened us. They were simply very, very poor. They were, maybe some of them, a little damaged by smoking the ever-present ganja weed of the islands—their only escape. We shouldn't be afraid, we agreed. They meant us no harm. We decided to go back to a little café on the beach and contribute to their economy. Ben and Jack did not want to go. We asked Ben to ferry us over and we would call him on the handheld radio when it was time to be picked up, so we wouldn't have to leave the dinghy on the beach unattended.

As our dinghy came in through the surf, a big wave caught us and sent us into the water. By the time we got things right, we realized it was going to be impossible for Ben to come back and get us, so we headed back to *Emerald Jane.* Sure enough, the raggedy man who had been on the sailboard had returned to the boat, probably lying low on his board so we wouldn't see him. He was up on the deck talking to little Jack.

Jack wasn't particularly worried; he would have put the interesting man in a jar if he could.

John cut the outboard and glided up, clutching an oar in his right hand, his anger close to exploding.

"Get ... *off* ... our boat," John growled in a low voice.

The man ignored him, turning back toward Jack.

John lifted the oar like a war club.

"Go," he said once more.

The man turned to stare at us; his bloodshot eyes had narrowed to hateful slits. But he then slid overboard like a magician and was gone.

After a tense meal in the cockpit, John went forward and positioned himself low on the trampoline between the bows. He would keep watch for the night—it was too dark to sail.

The rest of us went to bed. The boat was silent, but every time John shifted his weight, I could hear the trampoline web creaking above.

He scanned the black cove with our big binoculars. At his side was the flare gun, loaded with an exploding star shell round; it would be like shooting a Fourth of July rocket at someone—their grand finale.

The men came silently paddling toward the boat at half-past midnight.

We hadn't really heard any pirate violence stories at that time, and these weren't pirates in the most violent sense. John figured, rightly or wrongly, that they were more like aqua-burglers who probably expected to steal a few things as we slept. But who knows what they wanted? Who knows *who* they wanted? Who knows what they would be prepared to do if we tried to stop them?

John snapped on the hot beam of our biggest flashlight when they were as close as he wanted them to come. "Go, turn around now, or I *will* fire."

The flare pistol showed in the light for them to see. It looked like a handheld cannon. They silently turned and dissolved into the dark. A long night followed for John. We sailed at first light.

The stories of well-armed, speedboat-equipped, and utterly ruthless pirates from the Colombian and Venezuelan coasts kept us an extra hundred miles offshore as we skirted the northern brow of South America, heading first for Aruba. It argued for guns on board, too, but we resisted that. Yacht folks are pretty evenly divided on that issue. With kids aboard, we thought the danger would be greater with guns than without. We were a fast boat, which gave us some comfort.

John and Ben watched the radar every moment. We kept in radio contact with Steffan, but neither of us would disclose our positions for fear of being overheard and overtaken. The men had worked out a code for describing our positions, but we did not need to use it, at least not yet.

The *Emerald Jane* regrouped with the *Fruity Fruits* in Aruba, at the Seaport Marina in Oranjestad, the capital, only twenty-five miles from the Venezuelan mainland. After mapping out the next miles, the two crews set sail for the deadliest of the pirate waters.

A strange voice came over the radio: "Westbound vessels tracking 278 degrees, please respond." I searched the horizon but saw nothing. "Westbound vessels tracking 278 degrees," the voice repeated, "please respond and identify yourselves." John crossed the cockpit, went to the chart table, and picked up the microphone. "Go ahead channel 16, please identify *yourself.*"

"We are a British research vessel," the answer came back. "Standing by for your response." *Doesn't sound very British to me.* John answered, "This is the sailing vessel *Emerald Jane.*" The reply was immediate, insistent. "Sailing vessel *Emerald Jane,* please give your position, nationality, and registration number." Legitimate research vessels didn't have any business asking those kinds of questions. So he answered, "Research vessel, we don't recognize you or your jurisdiction."

The invisible ship then demanded the same information from *Fruity Fruits,* but Carolyne defiantly told them she would give neither her boat's name nor position. The radio hissed with the normal background static, and, for several minutes, the mysterious vessel was silent. The radio speaker sounded again. "*Emerald Jane,* this is an *armed* British research vessel." This was getting weird. Would pirates announce if they were armed—and who cared about a British research vessel, armed or otherwise?

Carolyne, tense because of the boats' location so near Colombia, came back on the radio and told the strange voice to "stop asking stupid questions." I was extremely nervous too and, in hope that the voice would go away, got on the same radio channel and proceeded to discuss what we were going to make for dinner, how her day was going, and what the kids were up to. When we finally ended our conversation the voice came back on the radio and identified themselves as the U.S. Coast

Guard, and the tone of voice implied they were tired of this game and meant business.

We gave them the information they wanted except for our positions, which we knew they already had and we didn't want to say aloud in case there were pirates listening on the same frequency. Carolyne recited *Fruity Fruits'* British registration number. In about fifteen minutes the Coast Guard cleared them to proceed. But the *Emerald Jane*, an American vessel, required more than an hour to be cleared.

It had been very strange—eerie even—to be questioned by an unknown voice over the radio on an empty sea, hundreds of miles from anywhere. We continued sailing and never saw the Coast Guard ship. John and I both stared at the horizon with binoculars and watched the radar screen, which should pickup a vessel up to sixteen miles away, but there was nothing. We were just getting ready to sit down to dinner when we heard the distinctive thrump, thrump, thrump, of a big helicopter. A tiny dot emerged from the overcast horizon, growing alarmingly larger and louder until it suddenly dropped and hovered over us. It was a flat-black military chopper, dark and unmarked. In a large, open door, a man with a very big machine gun stood with a dead expression. Other armed men stood around him. John saluted them and mumbled, "Ben, do *not* give them the finger." We suspected they were looking for either drug runners or pirates who had been eluding them. A surge of relief washed over me. The U.S. Coast Guard was in the area if we needed them. John didn't share my feelings. I could tell the incident troubled him.

At 10:00 that night, John had the watch. On the radar, he picked up the smudged green blip of a vessel following us at a distance of seven miles. It was too small to be something benign like a Coast Guard cutter. It didn't respond to radio calls.

Who are these guys? John was concerned it might be the pirates who had been eluding the Coast Guard. Within an hour, the maddening blip had closed to six miles. John changed course to see how the blip would react.

It changed course to follow. He reached up to the breaker panel and turned off the running lights, then made another big turn in the dark. For two minutes, the green blip seemed to be holding its original track. Then it swung onto *Emerald Jane*'s new heading. It was definitely following us and would probably close on us by first light.

John called Steffan and they used the code to see how far apart we were. *Fruity Fruits* was too far west to pick up the chasing ship on radar. They would try to close distance.

"Just keep all your lights off," Steffan said, "and hold this channel open."

John again changed course and the blip again followed suit. The kids and I were asleep; John was making decisions alone.

The only way out would be to use the catamaran's full potential for speed against the wind. You might think the last thing you would want to do would be to turn into the wind and thereby into the crashing swells of the sea, but going the wrong way like that is something old *Jane* could do pretty well, and the wrong-way sea swells could slow and bash the breezes out of a lesser ship following. He also started both turbo-charged diesels and ran them at full throttle, pushing *Emerald Jane* from eight to fourteen knots and about knocking us out of our bunks.

Amelia and I, groggy but alert to the ominous meaning of this, were soon braced in the cockpit door.

"What's up, Dad?"

"Not sure, honey."

"Pirates?" she guessed.

"Maybe."

The blip had closed within five miles, and again changed course to follow. Then, ever so slowly, the ghostly blip lagged on the radar screen.

At first light, we had pancakes instead of pirates.

"Nice work, Dad," Ben offered over the table after the full report.

Some hours after Amelia and I had gone back below that night, John went over to his prayer spot on the starboard deck and offered thanks for our safety.

I looked over to that spot now. The fallen mast was nearly off the deck, as the deck itself was being chewed away by the reef. The whole starboard side was now a mulch of boat bits and rigging, rising and falling in the waves with the hopelessly tangled lifeboat. We were perched on the only substantial part of the boat remaining.

At 1:30 a.m., Ben said he was going to leave us for a while. He dropped into the surf to go find the small patch of exposed reef he had spotted from time to time as the moon moved between clouds. The little shelf seemed to always be above water. When the moon came out each time, he would look to find it, and it would still be there above the waves.

He carried with him the flashing beacon and the heavy plastic case of flares. Ben knew that everybody, now perched on the ever-smaller stern, would soon have to abandon ship, and we would need a place to go.

The little ledge was a foot higher than the surrounding tidal pools. It was a flat spot about the size and shape of a parking space where coral could not grow higher for lack of constant contact with the sea and its nutrients. While its top was smooth, its edges were saw-blade sharp. He set down the heavy flare case and wedged the beacon upright into a crevice. Its red light, plus a nearly spent glow stick, would be our guide through the dark.

Ben hauled himself back on deck, exhausted from fighting the surf through the forest of razor coral. He said it was time to go. His legs were bleeding.

"Okay, Camille," he said. "We're going for a ride."

Camille clung to him, hiding her face in the hollow of his neck as he slid back into the water.

"I lost my shoes!" Jack yelled. He was worried about walking on the sharp coral.

"Come on, Jack," Amelia said. "I'll carry you."

She clamped Jack's legs around her left hip and took a deep breath, and they dropped into the dark sea. I watched my four children struggle away through the wild surf toward the faint glow of Ben's camp.

John was awash in his pain. He was bitterly cold. His ruined leg and bare feet dangled down the aft steps. I tried to warm him, protect him from the worst of the cold spray as we watched our children go.

Yes, you worry forever and you take a thousand precautions and there it is finally: all four of your children in the water, abandoning ship, struggling on a reef, far from anywhere in the middle of the South Pacific in the dead of night. Good job, Mom. I don't know if I was crying; there was too much stinging salt in the blast of the surf for me to hear myself or feel my tears. But, my God, watching them! Watching them clinging to each other, disappearing in the dark!

John looked briefly, and he could not speak—he was too weak. I chafed his hands and cheeks as he sat hunched forward. A weak glow of moonlight came through the clouds.

I begged him to say something, as he needed to remain conscious to stay alive.

"Hurts," he finally managed through his chattering teeth.

He was using the pain as creatively as he could to stay awake. He imagined a dentist's drill had gotten loose in his leg. He could hear it and smell it. He focused on this experience. He embraced the pain. He became one with it. It was the new him. There was some kind of new existence in this that he could explore to remain conscious, to keep the inviting voices away. He could tell them he didn't care to be comfortable, thank you; he would rather explore this pain, this almost religious ecstasy. He was in a new dimension.

Amelia waded back from the reef camp in the brightening moonlight. She offered to stay with John while I helped set up the camp. She thought I needed to be moving around—I was shivering, too. So I set off through the water toward the glow of the ledge.

[10]

ANOTHER DAY IN PARADISE

At the camp, I stripped off Camille's soaking clothes and Jack's wet T-shirt. Ben had moved some things to the camp, including floating cushions from the cockpit, which I told Jack and Camille to sit on, away from the coral's edges.

Ben arrived with another load of treasures.

"How are we going to get him off the boat?" I asked.

"Well," Ben said, his voice nervous with adrenaline, "the three of us will just have to carry him."

"Not with this surf," I said. "Not in the dark with these deep holes in the coral." One wrong step and John would be gone.

"I don't know how else to do it, Mom," Ben replied.

"We have to free the life raft," I said.

"It's too tangled, Mom. And I don't want to leave Jack and Camille here alone, in case a really big one breaks over the reef."

"I'm going back to watch your father," I said. I was really going back to free the raft.

Back on the boat, John was trying to stay conscious.

"He'll say a few words sometimes, but just like 'yes' or 'okay,' " Amelia reported.

I climbed over the wreckage along the starboard hull. The raft, gripped in the embrace of the jackknifed hull, looked hopelessly tangled in the rigging. I slipped into the surf. Waves rolled in between the broken bow section and the starboard hull, lifting me and sending me underwater with nearly every wave. I pushed and pulled, but the raft would not move.

The moon came and went from behind the clouds, revealing the reef and the Gordian knot before me every few minutes. I used every muscle in every combination, but pushing the raft more over here made it tangle more over there—a puzzle that would take all of whatever strength I had stored in my body from who knows how many morning runs, who knows how many swims and workouts along the way. This was it. This, I told myself, was life or death for John and maybe for all of us. I had to do this.

And so, my concentration on the raft, on the tangles, on the tightening grip of the broken hull, viciously consumed me. Waves caught me off guard constantly, coming at me from every angle, filling my nose and mouth with salt water. I coughed and vomited it out, hanging on to the edge of the deck or a tight cable for a few seconds each time, then going back at it, back under the water, stretching my legs in some new attack, literally punching the rubber bulges up through another tangle—an inch at a time. I perceived a trade-off developing: The more I budged the raft out of its bondage, the more tangled I myself became. I was spending too much time underwater, tangled and pressed into tight places. There was nothing anyone could do to help me right now; this was a puzzle for one, and anyone else would only have made it more complicated. I struggled against incredible cramps in my legs. I gulped for air between waves.

Maybe some shark would come help me. Maybe he would miss my

leg in the dark and cut a rope or two, and we would get this thing done. I felt my mind spinning away from its rational center. This was a fury of muscle and mind and it was all from a different part of the brain. This was about survival. I was an animal, struggling under one wave for my mate and my offspring, and under the next for myself. I thought I could not go on much longer, but then, with a second wind, I somehow believed I could go on for days—that this is what life is.

I needed more energy and better luck. This was not working. I pulled myself free and waded through the surf and coral to our camp. I carefully climbed up to rest. I had been hyperventilating. My whole body was in spasms. I steadied my breathing and my thoughts. I waited for the moon. I then swam back and tried using my legs more, holding on to the hull and pushing the jackknifed bow away with my legs. The bow again seemed to move a little from the hull—a little more and perhaps the raft would pop free. I could see the raft shift. *Just a little more,* I told myself. I pushed harder. I yelled for Ben to come cut the tightest lines. He was soon in the thick of them with the saw blade.

The raft popped free, shooting up like a great gray dolphin. It was deeply scarred by the squeeze of the broken boat and by the coral. The canopy was torn open, but the main ring of it was still inflated. Speedy the turtle and all our supplies were nowhere inside. My legs, like Ben's, were gashed by the coral and bleeding badly. You think about sharks when that happens. I decided to think about dolphins instead. The raft popping up had put them in my head for a second, and I brought them in to chase away my fear of sharks.

Dolphins were an easy thought for me—an indelible memory. I had a sense of them as real friends, beginning the day after John outran the pirates. Just after lunch that day, dolphins surrounded the *Emerald Jane* and raced and leapt across our wake. They had no trouble keeping up with our eight knots.

Jack and Camille saw them first: "Dolphins, you guys! Lots of dolphins! Hurry up!" The kids had been wrestling on the wide green trampoline between the twin bows.

Amelia put away her pastel-chalk landscape and ran forward. She called for everybody to come quickly.

A dolphin leapt high before the bow, beautifully.

"Dad, *man*! did you see him?" Jack bellowed. He switched to his sports announcer voice: "That boy's got *air*!"

Camille was on her stomach, looking through the big crisscross web of the trampoline to the water under the boat.

"Elebenteen!" she counted.

Amelia ran for the video camera.

"Look, Dad," Jack pointed, "a mom swimming with her babies!"

I counted thirty dolphins around us, and there were, as we knew, elebenteen or so under us. With the video camera, I crouched on the port bow and recorded the moment. John was so moved he was speechless in a blissful daze. This was what we had come for. How on earth is it that we build so many walls between us and the beauty of the world? Well, here we were at last.

Off to starboard, an unexpected second act: green sea turtles swam just beneath the surface. They sailed below the waves, faster than we every could have imagined, but no match for the *Emerald Jane* and the dolphins.

Ben, too, was moved to see it all. This was good. His moody resistance wouldn't end entirely for a very long time, but he let the beauty in. He had a big, silly smile; he was pointing at all the jumping dolphins with *ohhs* and *ahhs* and clapping with the rest of us.

"That one's talking!" Jack sang out, pointing to a large dolphin. "He's looking right at me!"

"Me, too!" Camille piped in.

I was wondering if they would start dancing backward on their fins, clicking away at us. I so wanted to click back to them.

Their brilliant synchronization to every move of the boat seemed a perfect modern ballet. Amelia, our ballerina, was unconsciously en pointe as she watched them. These creatures, whose brains are about the size of ours, know how to have a good time. No freeways. No grocery bills. No taxes. No rent or mortgage payments. They have it figured out, and they were trying to explain it to us. All we could do was smile and wave and yell our stupid mammal hellos. Maybe that's all they were doing, too.

John was just beaming. This was really it. Standing beside me, he pulled my hip into his and pecked my cheek.

"Another day in paradise, baby," he whispered.

The dolphins disappeared as quickly as they came. We fell quiet—even Jack and Camille. We are a religious family, but this was perhaps our first truly religious moment together. "Amazing, incredible, beautiful, awesome," were the various spontaneous prayers we shared as we stared at one another and the sea.

The moment of calm that I felt out on the bow after the mast fell was somehow a part of that feeling. I can't fully explain it. Dolphins die, too, but they are so beautiful that they are well worth the sadness of their mortality. Enough beauty redeems any pain, at least in time. Maybe the calm had come from knowing that John had not wasted his life, that he had done his great thing and been so beautiful.

In any event, the dolphins of my imagination were all around us as Ben and I pushed our bloody legs through the water. They were bouncers to keep any sharks out of this reef. We tugged and pushed the raft through the waves toward the port stern where John sat shivering, teetering in the spray, keeping his balance with Amelia's help as each wave rolled under the stern and blasted up from the engine compartment below them.

"Come on, Dad," Ben shouted, "just slide down. We've got the raft." Every effort had to be timed with the rise and fall of water.

John could not move or answer. You could see he understood and was trying, but his body was not following his commands. He would not accept that situation. With great effort, he supported himself down one step. From there, we carried him into the raft while Amelia steadied it against the swell and pull of the waves.

We towed the raft through the surf toward the reef, using each new wave to boost the raft over the next sharp outcropping. At the foot of the camp ledge was a tidal pool that seemed a calm enough harbor. It would be best to leave John in the raft, where he had some cover. I sent near-naked Jack and Camille inside to clamp themselves around their father. They lay there in the blood with him. Amelia stood chest-deep in the lagoon, holding the raft clear of the coral ledge. She watched the moonlit water around her for sharks.

Ben and I watched a high breaker roll over the *Emerald Jane* and take her finally apart. There was not enough hull left below to support her decks; she twisted into the sea. Thanks to Ben, we had left in time, and not by many minutes.

It hadn't been that long ago that he was an angry and sometimes mean kid. Now I was looking at Ben the man. It hadn't happened all at once, but it had happened.

After that afternoon of the dolphins, when we were still running from pirates, the weather turned suddenly treacherous and I got my first glimpse of Ben coming into manhood.

It was 3:00 in the afternoon when high winds rose astern. An hour later John told Ben the wind was averaging twenty-two knots with higher gusts.

Ben knew it would soon be necessary to reef the sails—meaning that the big sail would be lowered a bit and the genoa would be cranked in a ways. That's what you have to do in too much wind. His adolescent stubbornness briefly reappeared; he didn't look in the mood for the hard work. But high clouds were flying where there had been only blue sky two hours before, leaving no doubt.

John called me to come up and help.

"Let's go, Ben," John ordered as captain.

"Dad, we don't need a reef."

"It's going to be dark soon, Ben. And it's going to blow harder, so it's *now*."

John switched off the autopilot; I took the wheel; Ben took his place at the mast. I waited for the signal to bring the big cat into the wind, which would take the pressure off the sails long enough for them to be cranked down a bit. Everything must be performed quickly once the turn begins.

John gave the order. As the boat came about, we could feel the full force of the wind we had been riding. The men worked the sails perfectly.

Watching them work so expertly together was a big moment for me: Two men were working on the foredeck. My little boy had grown up.

We steered a course far out from the pirate coast of the Guajira Peninsula. The 16,000-foot mountains of that peninsula make the winds as treacherous as the pirates.

After dinner, John always took a little nap, as his normal watch ran all through the night.

"Dad, you need to check things out." It was past seven, still Ben's watch, but Ben was leaning over John's face to wake him.

"Something on the radar?"

"No, it's the wind, coming up *hard*."

Out in the dark cockpit, John could feel *Emerald Jane* laboring to hold her course.

"Check it out." Ben waved him forward on the port deck, and together they leaned outboard just as the bow clipped off the top two feet of a wave. They ducked under the bimini as the wave washed across the deck and spilled overboard.

"It feels like we've got too much sail up," Ben continued. "The wind's never below twenty-five."

We had too much genoa exposed for this wind and sea; it was tilting the boat forward, driving the twin bows under the waves instead of over them.

"We'll stay on our course and furl in half the genny," John said.

Ben acknowledged and turned to get the winch handle.

"That's *my* job!" little Jack yelled as he came aft from the salon.

"Go ahead, Jack," John said. "But have four turns on that winch before you open the sail stop, or it'll pop and pull your hand off." The eight-year-old understood exactly.

John and Ben watched as Jack worked his way carefully forward, inserted the crank and pulled with all his might. The wind on the sail was too much. It took both Ben and John to move the sail. It made Jack feel a little better to see that no one could do it by himself.

Ninety minutes later, Steffan called to say that the *Fruity Fruits,* forty miles away by our secret code, was having a hard time of it. I took the call from him, as I often did, with Ben feeding me our position. Steffan seemed calm, but there was something in his voice: This storm was rising and he seemed worried. His autopilot couldn't hold the rudder and it kept kicking out—that takes a lot of wind and sea. Our own boat was lurching wildly. We were in a gale.

I was on watch at the wheel, wearing my yellow foul-weather jacket, even though the bimini still afforded decent protection—John had built it strong. The jacket was necessary when you jumped up on the higher deck around the cockpit to scan the horizon for ships and other obstacles, which must be done regularly. A soaking spray was now pounding the decks.

Our twin bows were plunging deeper and deeper into the waves—dangerously so.

John went forward to trim in the rest of the genoa. It took all his strength to roll up the 250 square feet of sail against the full force of the wind.

That helped. I turned over the watch to John, with the boat behaving a little better but the sea still rising.

The *Emerald Jane* was essentially surfing the huge waves, always just ahead of their towering, breaking crests. John tensed as each big one began curling up above him, just twenty feet astern. He would look up into the surf cascading down the face of the wave, and he braced for the certain impact, but that impact was always averted at the last moment as the stern rose up and away on the advancing sea. One wrong move, however, and we would be in trouble, swamped by a wave as tall as a building.

The wind speed increased and the waves towered higher than he had seen before, ever. At times, *Emerald Jane* was racing down the face of the waves at fourteen knots, slowing to ten at the bottom, then picking up again and riding high into the night sky, then down again.

By sailing necessity, we were slowly closing with the dangerous coast of Colombia. The phosphorescence and roar of the sea as it rose up and tumbled behind us was breathtaking. I could not sleep in this chaos, but John was fine with all of it.

Shortly after 10:00, the autopilot was overpowered and couldn't hold course; the warning beep was barely audible over the gale. John was adjusting the main sheet when it happened. By the time he reached the wheel, the boat had started a slow turn to port as we rose out of a trough. Disaster was seconds away, but he turned her back into a safe slide down the wave. The autopilot had luckily failed in the trough, the safest moment in the wave sequence. Otherwise, we could have turned sideways and rolled into the sea—submerged and crushed in the blink of an eye.

Anyone still asleep was soon awake when the failure of the autopilot caused the mainsail to take the full wind. Amelia rushed out to the cockpit and yelled over the storm to find out what happened. John shouted back the explanation.

The gale strengthened, reaching a shrieking intensity. Carolyne radioed from the *Fruity* to tell me they got hit by a monster wave. She sounded freaked. When these pro sailors worry, then I worry. I ran to convey the message to John. He could see I was shaken as I rushed through the wild cockpit to the wheel. We were like bugs on a ship in a bottle, and the bottle was being shaken hard. Just standing up was incredibly difficult.

"Shouldn't we call the Coast Guard or something?" I yelled to him from a foot away.

He took his eye off the sea breaking behind us. "We're okay. Stay calm," he winked.

The gusts increased to forty-five knots.

Just before midnight, I went back out to John. Amelia was with me. I held out the satellite phone to him.

"John, you have *got* to call the Coast Guard right now." Amelia seconded the motion with her terrified look.

"All right, okay. I'll call and fill them in. Give me the phone."

The call went through: "... Normal business hours are eight a.m. until five p.m., Monday through Friday..."

He kept that to himself and shouted our position into the phone.

"This is the American sailing vessel *Emerald Jane,* our position is twelve degrees, fourteen minutes north, and seventy-eight degrees, thirty-two minutes west. Please note our position as of 03:44 U.T.C. We are in a full gale, and will contact you again should we require assistance. Thank you."

No message machine was on the line, but he didn't mention that, either. He saw some relief in our faces.

Amelia crossed the rolling cockpit again, this time in her yellow foul-weather jacket.

"Dad, are we going to be okay?"

"Absolutely."

"Yes, but really?"

"Do you trust me to tell you the truth?"

She paused and then nodded yes.

"We're fine."

The wind and sea continued to rise. John was looking back con-

stantly, just as a surfer watches the wave building behind. We were surfing for our lives. The air filled with scattered spray and spindrift foam.
The sea lifted *Emerald Jane* higher than before and flung her forward—the
wheel spun away from his grip. He grabbed it in spin and held his body
hard to it.

The twin bows were now sewing through the tops of the waves, disappearing with each stabbing entry. Our speed went to fourteen, then fifteen, then eighteen knots. Then we were flying down cliffs of seawater
into black canyons, impossibly steep, impossibly deep. The boat rum-
bled with a deep bass pounding; the wind gauge jumped past forty-five
knots.

If our bows should bury too deep in the waves, the *Emerald Jane* could
flip, stern over bow.

Steering the boat became an intense meditation for John; it would
not admit the slightest error of judgment. Twenty knots now. The hulls,
the rigging, the rudders, even the cockpit boards were vibrating in a new
way. John imagined this was prelude to the arrival of a rogue wave, the
mysterious monsters that can make even big tankers disappear in a
blink.

Our speed was out of control. John realized we had to drop the main.
We would have to go out there on that wild foredeck and get the big sail
down—incredibly dangerous. We would have to turn the ship into the
teeth of these waves to do it, taking the pressure off the sail for the seconds needed to lower some canvas.

It was just too easy to lose a child with this. He called me out to take
the wheel. He started the engines to give some control for the maneuver.

"I'll wave to you," he yelled, inches from my ear to be heard. "And then
you make the turn. The second the main drops, swing back downwind."
I nodded, soaked, blasted by the foam.

"Clip on," I shouted, meaning the safety tether along the deck. "Be
careful."

He crept forward, inching against the cabin sides, stopping and holding on with both hands when he had to. He made his preparations with the lines and gave me a big wave. The *Emerald Jane* flew off the top of a wave and smashed into the back of another. The breaking waves stalled the boat in midturn. Worse, a batten of the sail—a rib stiffener—caught in the rigging and was holding the sail up. The main wouldn't drop.

"Go again!" he screamed and waved.

I turned the wheel to starboard, and we bashed our way back downwind, sliding sideways down a wave. I turned the boat back into the fury to give John another shot, but through the foam I saw him slip and fall as a wave swept the deck. The mainsail began to flog violently, which miraculously freed it from its tangle. John released the main halyard, and the sail slipped down into its folds on the boom. I swung us back with the waves aft. John came back to the wheel and we kissed. Such a fine and salty kiss from that old man! I felt welded to him in that kiss. We *did* need each other, terribly and always.

We flew through the night, remaining ever just out of the ocean's claws. A wave swept over the boat, swirling in the cockpit. Carolyne radioed to say a wave had covered them, but Steffan held on and was okay.

I shouted the news out to John, shocked by the sight of high water in the cockpit.

"Another day in paradise, baby," he shouted back.

By 1:00 a.m., wind speeds across the deck were fifty knots—often fifty-five. John looked forward in wonder at the waves, the products of a full force-10 storm. Some were easily thirty feet—three stories—high.

After 2:00 a.m., the storm weakened.

Ben, who had been knocked unconscious by seasickness medicine for much of the ride, heard the details in the morning and was much impressed with his father and maybe a little with his mother. I saw him looking at his father with a very fine stare. Respect so helps a child grow up—both the receiving and the giving of it.

As the autopilot was clearly shot, the question now was whether to go somewhere for lengthy repairs, or just keep going, with every mate taking a real turn at the wheel, not just monitoring the autopilot.

Ben physically stepped forward: "No sweat, Dad, we can do it."

Amelia was good with it. Jack, of course, wouldn't have it any other way, and Camille was ready to learn the wheel, even if it meant climbing it.

We held our heading toward the Panama Canal and the wide Pacific.

Yes, we can handle stuff now, I was thinking. That feeling had stayed with me through the months to come. It was with me even on the reef, in the raft, holding John. Whatever was going to happen, this family would just handle it. We had learned that.

[11]

SEEING THINGS

Hours and hours passed, and Amelia would not budge from holding the raft. When the moon went behind clouds, she could not watch for sharks so she had to think about other things and hope for the best.

"Maybe there is an island," she said to me, "with islanders who'll come find us."

I didn't think so: They certainly had not been impressed by the flares we shot at the moon.

"Maybe they go to bed early," Amelia replied to my silent doubt.

"Maybe so."

I imagined what might happen if this were indeed some spit of real land. Maybe there would be a few coconut palms. Maybe we could collect rainwater and catch fish. I would surely be taking care of the kids alone. And for how long? A day? A week? Longer?

We were all fighting hypothermia. I had taken off my yellow storm jacket and draped it across John and the babies. I was down to a T-shirt and a pair of shorts.

Amelia slid neck-deep into the tidal pool to escape the chill wind. Colorful parrot fish swam around her in the moonlight.

I lay down inside the raft with John and the kids, trying to share what little warmth remained in my body. I rubbed his waxen flesh. Inside were a few inches of water. I bailed it out, spilling his blood into the water around Amelia. She has always been afraid of sharks. Ben will swim with them, but not Amelia.

"Keep your eye out, okay," I reminded her.

"I will, Mom."

"If one comes up, you are supposed to hit them hard on the nose."

"Okay, Mom."

I tried to think about dolphins instead of sharks, but it was no use. Sharks. John dying. Sharks.

Sailors used to call sharks "sea dogs." I like that a lot better when you're in the water and they're maybe around. They're hungry old dogs that happen to have, yes, pretty good choppers. Their teeth are so rock-hard that they're the only thing left of them when they die; they don't have much of a skeleton other than cartilage and some bony bits. But their teeth last on the ocean bottom for millions of years—always the cheapest thing in a fossil store. Sometimes the males use those teeth to hold the females during mating. Wisely, some females sharks have been found to develop very thick skin. Even wiser, some have been found to reproduce asexually. Sharks are not as dangerous as most people fear, but you don't want to stand around in a reef bleeding—we were really asking for it. They can hear for miles, and John was a wounded animal making sounds into the water. They can smell for miles. Blood is their specialty, and they're sensitive to one part per million. They are sensitive, perhaps alone among animals, to the electrical fields animals give off. So a fish hiding under the sand is still on their scope. The electrical features of boats are known to attract them, and all our wires and batteries were probably sending out invitations for twenty miles around. So we watched.

Ben, scrounging the area for useful flotsam from the wreck, came up with a packet containing a foil emergency blanket. We wrapped it tightly around John. He still shook uncontrollably; his monosyllables were incoherent.

Ben returned with a chunk of watermelon and a plastic bottle of cola. He leaned into the raft and smiled at John.

"You're gonna make it, Dad," he said.

John nodded his answer, his face rigid.

In the moonlight, the reef looked otherworldly to me. Yet it was our planet—so remarkably beautiful. I could see a curve to the reef—a great circle with a lagoon in the center. Such a reef, an atoll, forms around the shoreline of an ancient volcanic island. As the volcano erodes over millions of years, the crusty coral remains in conelike cliffs that reach down to the distant ocean floor.

The reef is tiny animals. They take the calcium from the sea, as do all the shellfish, and make little homes. They die and leave their caves behind, as we leave our skeletons. So many life and death events, a reef surely is. Such a pile of it, a mile high. And all along it, if we could go down with our masks and our tanks and some lights, it is so incredibly beautiful. So many colors—animals like flying saucers and neon animals. The colors are wild but perfectly suited to each little work of art. They depend on this pile of skeletons, and on the violent volcano that began their world.

John Muir, of my California, called the violence of nature a kind of "beauty-making"—like the avalanches that styled Yosemite's cliffs and domes and waterfalls. Well, then, what beauty was being made here? How would my kids be stronger and wiser and more beautiful on account of this? And John? And me? Our marriage? Was this long night intent on making some new beauty of us, or just snuffing us out so it might have the calcium from our bones?

But for minutes or an hour more, we are not dead in the water in some

Rancho Sargasso subdivision. By God, we are here, teetering on the edge of an ancient volcano after two years of one leap of faith after another. Did we think we could survive forever? Might we please do so at least tonight?

For so much of our lives, we are afraid to really live—afraid not only to burn the candle at both ends, but even afraid to burn one end for fear we will burn it all up someday. And yes, Life is a death trap. But that's all right: The whole thing is just beautiful. We were under attack by the ancient skeletons of the sea, and you had to admit the beauty of that.

As the dawn light finally came, John still prayed for us. We had switched things around: Jack and Camille were sitting on the reef. Ben was still finding supplies that might be useful for our survival. Amelia was inside the raft to keep John warm; this was not an easy thing to do, as the raft was filled with a soup of seawater, blood, vomit, and pee. She lay down in it next to John. That is love.

John's low prayers were all he could manage now; he did not answer us. I held the raft steady in the lagoon.

I kept seeing things that were not there: A distant jag of coral became a boat in my mind; a bird in the predawn was, I thought, an airplane.

"You're dehydrated, Mom," Amelia told me. She made me drink from one of the water bottles Ben had recovered.

I watched the morning of our new world arrive. The idea of John leaving us on this day—leaving me this new day—was impossibly sad. The litter of our life, washing up in the low tide under the moon, was so remarkable to see. Our shipwreck as a family had been our isolation from the beauty of our world and from each other. We had rescued ourselves from that, but at what price? If we were to lose John and he were to lose his life?

I knew John was dying. I didn't know the details, but you cannot lose as much blood as he had lost, you couldn't be as cold that long and have an open wound sponging up a bacterial soup, and not soon slip away. Indeed, I would learn, he was suffering acute renal failure; his kidneys had begun shutting down within minutes of the original injury. And during the three hours he was trapped beneath the mast his body and blood were poisoned by the now complete collapse of his kidneys. He had lost more than half his blood already. Other organs were shutting down. Kidneys now, followed soon by liver, lungs, and central nervous system. He would cross the threshold into full-blown septic shock and likely die before midmorning. I understood all that somehow without knowing the medical details.

The wind was still cold, and I was freezing. But the water in the tidal pool felt warm, and I snuggled deep into it. What a strange, dark passage in our lives! I let the warmth of the lagoon comfort me.

There was a scent of diesel fuel in the water as the boat dissolved further. Those beautiful engines that John so prized were now rolling in the coral along with the new generator we had bought in Panama.

We bought it through a distributor. It was installed at a yacht club that was secured by barbed wire and armed guards—protected from the poverty around it. What an eye-opener that had been for the kids! Panama, dreamlike and nightmarish. The city at the eastern canal opening is Colón. In this dream are the towering, rusty gates of the canal's locks; clanking electric locomotives pulling immense container ships through the mosquito heat; powerful eddies of greasy water lifting the huge freighters and little sailboats.

Through the locks, the *Emerald Jane* was lashed—"rafted"—between two other sailboats, a French forty-five-footer on starboard and an English thirty-eight-foot boat on the port side. Through those first locks and then freed of the raft, we sailed through a necklace of lakes to the Pacific locks, steering between jungle-draped mountains.

As we motored down lake Gatun and found an overnight anchorage, the dead air was heavy and hot. This was not the place to take a swim, however, as hundreds of crocodiles churned the water around us. Sweating, fanning myself on deck, I thought about Kate Hepburn and Mr. Bogart in *The African Queen,* and that somehow cheered me. We sweated there, waiting our turn to go through the second set of mammoth, rusty locks that would release us into the wide Pacific.

In these humid days of waiting, we went ashore with the Van Zwams to explore. We journeyed up the Chagres River by motorboat through the steamy rain forest, and then by Jeep to the cool Boquete Highlands. We hiked through clouds along mountain trails. We were in no hurry; we had no better place to be.

I took Amelia horseback riding. She enjoyed it so much that, for the few weeks we anchored in Panama City, she often rode after finishing her schoolwork.

When the new generator had been tested to John's satisfaction, we sailed with *Fruity Fruits* into the Pacific. We wanted to head to Cocos Island, where Ben said he could dive among hammerhead sharks. He generally liked dangerous fish, although he'd been afraid of a particular barracuda back in Tortola that was as big as he was. Ben had moved faster back to the boat on that occasion than I'd thought possible. Jack wanted to go to Cocos for his own reason: He said *Jurassic Park* had been filmed there and maybe some dinosaurs were still left. But the winds weren't going that way. When your home is a sailboat, you learn to go with the winds.

We tied up instead off a sandy beach on Isla Gobernadora, with dense jungles just beyond the sand. The anchorage in this Pacific cove was dreamlike. After all the traffic din and teeming street markets of Panama City, this return to the prehistoric tropics was somehow like coming home. We heard children's voices in the jungle as we stepped from the dinghy onto the beach. The air was scented with unseen citrus blossoms.

A woman with a warm smile approached me with a gift of freshly cut coconut. Camille was soon wading in the long surf with shy brown girls her own age. A group of very young boys materialized and cautiously surrounded Jack, intrigued by his blond hair and white skin. They were all in the water an instant later, hunting small octopi from under ledges of coral; they held the tentacled creatures high to show us. It was an idyllic day.

The next morning, John was in the cockpit drinking coffee, finishing a papaya, and writing in his log. Jack had sprinkled bread crumbs on the stern steps and had some gulls for company. A black rubber Zodiac attack boat slowly moved toward *Emerald Jane.* A soldier on the bow of the intimidating boat trained an M60 machine gun at John, who carefully set down his coffee and slowly stood up. John expected this was the notorious National Maritime Service division of the "FPP," which had a shoot-first reputation for drug interdiction work. Other men aboard were clutching Uzi machine guns and pointing them at our boat. The helmsman, swinging the boat into ours, had a MAC-10 machine pistol.

They tied up at our stern. Their commander, unholstering his gun, stepped aboard without asking permission. Machine guns do make people rude. John could see into their inflatable boat, which was littered deep with spent brass shell casings.

John greeted him in Spanish, asking how he could help.

The man demanded *Emerald Jane's* papers. A couple of the boys in the patrol boat now watched the shore, but the rest continued to stare at John. Then Camille and Jack appeared from down below and softened the tension. Ben came up to stare back at the men. The cockpit remained dead-still while I brought *Emerald Jane's* document folder up. John winked at me as he took it, and, speaking in Spanish, offered the captain a chair.

In Spanish, the captain grilled John for a while: nationality, number of crew, destination, home port.

"La Ciudad de San Diego," John said.

The Panamanian grinned. His cousin was playing baseball at San Diego State.

As the conversation warmed, John asked about the spent cartridges in their boat. They had shot up some Colombian drug runners outside of Las Perlas. His crew smiled and laughed as he recounted the massacre.

The captain then rose abruptly and thanked me for the coffee. He knew we were planning to head next to the Galápagos, so he gave us a warning. He spoke in broken English for my benefit.

"Be careful down there. Stay clear of Isla de Malpelo—big drug people meet up there and the men are very, very bad. *Muy malo, Señora.*" He touched the bill of his hat to me, and he departed.

Stories of boat hijackings were as numerous around Panama as they had been in the Caribbean. John and Ben had put together a defense plan, just in case we ever needed it. Gas cans were kept in the storage space beneath the cockpit. In an emergency, Ben and John would fetch them from beneath the cockpit floor, open them, then, as the invaders approached, heft the cans toward or even into their boat, igniting the gas with flare guns. If it didn't work, it would at least have been a spectacular effort. And why not? We would be cooked anyway.

Jack wanted in on the action, but he decided he would have his hands full protecting Speedy the turtle and his other charges. He'd become *Emerald Jane's* unofficial biologist. Ashore or in the water, he was always the expert on what was what. On our trip up the Chagres River, the monkeys and birds in the hardwood canopy all had names that he somehow knew. He had studied our tropical wildlife photo book and had memorized many of the creatures by their common and Latin names. There seemed to be very few creatures he couldn't name.

I looked at Jack now, sharing the coral ledge with his little sister. It wasn't enough for him to sit there waiting for rescue: He was on his hands and knees peering over the ledge to examine the life of the reef, of which he himself was perhaps the most colorful specimen.

Odd that perhaps it was little Jack who had come to this voyage best equipped to appreciate it. When, after Panama, we were heading to the

Galápagos, which are the richest biological nurseries on the planet, I figured he would be leading the way. Part of all this journey, in my mind, was about getting Jack to the Galápagos.

But the wind didn't want to go to the Galápagos when we did. It had Ecuador in mind. After consultation with the Van Z's on the radio, we changed course. Carolyne said there was a safe marina at Puerta Lucia near Salinas, Ecuador. From there, the Andean highlands would be a day's Jeep drive. Jack was fine with it.

We crossed the equator. You dress for that. John's head and shoulders were draped with fishnet. He wore a crown of crinkled aluminum foil and held up a fish gaff as his scepter. I was this King Neptune's handmaiden, wearing my black pirate head-scarf. It was my duty to serve up gross-looking slices of anchovies—the children's least favorite food. When crossing the equator, a ceremony is called for by sailing tradition and is referred to as "Crossing the Line."

"On this day, June 28, 2004, you have crossed the equator for the first time in your lives and have gone from lowly pollywogs to shellbacks. We are now in the Southern Hemisphere, and you are true mariners," the king proclaimed to the assembled deckhands.

Each of us wrote a private note to the deeper King Neptune, which we put in a bottle and delivered overboard. Everyone had to have a tiny bite from the plate of anchovies.

My own wish was that our family would find happiness always, and that John and I would always be together. I didn't know what was in store for us in the months to come, but the excitement of the unknown gave me a nervous stomach.

In the near term, I was looking forward to visiting South America, the Galápagos, the South Pacific, and then Australia. But beyond that? John alone in Australia was a worry to me, but I could think about that later—fiddledee dee. For now, please, no more worrying. This was a true adventure, and I was determined to leave behind my overly methodical mentality. I could not micromanage the South Pacific. I had accepted that plans were intended to change with the wind.

We made final offerings to the deep by tossing overboard a sprinkling of leftover Caribbean coins. Amelia proudly offered the sea a plate of cupcakes with chocolate frosting that she had baked early in the morning. We didn't think the sea would want all of them, as big as it already is, so we ate some of them ourselves. Amelia was baking every day now, as well as sewing clothes of her own design, making jewelry pendants from clay, and drawing seascapes in pastels and watercolors. Sunsets and palm trees were her specialties.

During the equator ceremony, we had been sailing through a cool, intimate fog, but shortly after the offerings, the fog cleared and we sailed for a time in a sphere of gauzy sunlight. Just as suddenly, we were surrounded by millions of leaping sardines in a shower of silver. Maybe it was a thanks for the silver we sent below. Then a school of iridescent, torpedolike bluefin tuna shot into the air, splashing on both sides of the boat. Jack spotted pilot whales off to starboard. The fog then drifted back over us.

At the ship's wheel, Amelia saw the distant Andes Mountains holding the red of sunset. Then they mysteriously disappeared before her eyes. She called her Dad out from the dinner table. By that time the mountains were back, but hovering high in the air over the horizon.

"They call it *fata morgana*," John told her, "after the trickster spirit from the King Arthur stories—Mordred's mother or aunt, depending on the version." Heat rising from the broad Andean coast had created the mirage.

Our family schoolroom soon moved to trails high in those mountains. Jack was fascinated by the llamas. Amelia and Ben explored an ancient Inca ruin with the Van Zwam kids.

Hiking through the Andean villages was a big moment for Amelia: She suddenly got it that there are other great ways to live on the planet—

beautiful, modest ways. It would change her. And her eye for design and fabric was getting an education. She had made friends on boats here and there in the Caribbean—particularly Lucy, whose boat had a sewing machine on board, a great revelation to Amelia. Amelia and Lucy made skirts together that Amelia now wore nearly every day. She never quite got the thrill of designer labels after that. She had discovered natural fibers, batik-printed fabrics, loose-fitting pirate wear, amazing colors.

In Panama, she and I found little stalls where the Kuna Indian women of San Blas sold their "mola" fabric for blouses, skirts, and tapestries. You have seen it: reverse appliqué created by layering fabric, then sewing their designs, then cutting out the top layers to expose the colored layers below. Typical motifs are geometric, mythological, biblical, animals and marine life. We had a Kuna woman make two wall hangings for the boat. One was a colorful underwater marine-life scene for Jack's room and the other was an eagle for Ben's room. Amelia came up with the idea of having the molas match the royal blues in Jack's room and the reds in Ben's.

Through all of this, the sight of hard work and poverty moved Amelia deeply. She had, down through the islands, been on fancy parties on yachts and she knew what that was all about. But if there was a temptation of Amelia on this adventure, her soul passed the test.

From Ecuador, we sailed six hundred miles to the Galápagos, where Darwin had observed the profusion of life that informed his theory of evolution. Because the islands are so isolated, plants and animals unlike any others had evolved and survived there.

The anchorage was narrow, dominated by arid volcanic hills layered with the red-tile roofs of nineteenth-century Spanish colonial buildings and modest cinder-block houses. The first order of business was an eye doctor for Ben, who had come down with a nasty conjunctivitis. The treatment, including the prescription, was about seven dollars. I had needed some stitches and medicine myself back in Ecuador, which had set us back ten dollars.

Our love of the sea made us choose a church and yacht club in Mamaroneck, New York, on Long Island Sound, to have our wedding. It was the same harbor where we would start our adventure seventeen years later.

Four Silverwood bachelors and their nervous parents. We were all married shortly. My father now complains about buying birthday presents for thirteen grandkids.

One of our most treasured photos of the *Emerald Jane*, anchored in the lagoon at Bora Bora. She was looking her very best with all the additions and changes we made to her.

Our favorite anchorage—Opunohu Bay, Moorea, a fantasy island out of a storybook. *Mutiny on the Bounty* was filmed here. Shark Tooth Mountain rises in the background.

Jack shows his cousin Brady "the ropes"—Norman Island, British Virgin Islands.

Fitting new canvas on the bimini above our cockpit in St. Thomas, U.S. Virgin Islands. A major headache at sea, but we finally fixed it using plenty of patience—and money!

Cooking was one of Amelia's favorite pastimes, even in such a small space. Many a gourmet meal was made in the galley. Stephanie Van Zwam is assisting the chef.

Ocean air makes for good appetites. Everyone had a job to do in getting dinner on the table. What we'd do and where we'd go for our next stop was always a topic.

(*Above*) Queen for a day in Aruba! Breakfast in bed followed by cards, gifts, and a wreck dive made for a Mother's Day I will never forget.

(*Left*) Isla Gobernadora, Panama. Jack is most at home in the water. He was our very own Darwin, always in search of a new species.

King Neptune at rest, having just initiated his crew through the ritual "Crossing the Line" ceremony. Crossing over the equator into the Southern Hemisphere had advanced our status as sailors from lowly pollywogs to one of hardened shellbacks (sea turtles). Pacific Ocean, latitude 0.00 degrees.

The lineup: Jack and his newfound friends finish searching for sea creatures and comparing notes in English and Spanish. Isla Gobernadora, Panama.

Camille found friends everywhere we went. It never mattered that they didn't speak the same language.

Horseback riding was a favorite mother/daughter outing, and we took advantage of it whenever possible. Resting our horses after a gallop through the pineapple fields in Moorea.

Ben doing a lab experiment in the salon. Later the results would be shipped stateside and graded by his teachers at school in California.

John passes his open water scuba diving test, St. Thomas, U.S. Virgin Islands. The rating opened a stunning world, enabling us and the older kids to experience unforgettable dives in the Caribbean and throughout the vast Pacific.

(*Right*) The kids insisted on the biggest Christmas tree we could fit on the boat, and lights, which we purchased in St. Martins. While in Bermuda we bought some beautiful blown-glass ornaments to hang on the tree.

(*Below*) *Survivor* Bequia! Jack and Amelia hard at play building a real tree house they dreamed up just above the beach in the oldest whaling island of the southern Caribbean.

Jack never missed a chance to dive for surprises and never met a reef he didn't like.
Here he's bringing back a live octopus he found in the huge lagoon of Manihi,
Tuamotus Archipelago, French Polynesia.

Jack and Camille watch as the locks of the Panama Canal open to the Pacific Ocean and the
adventures ahead.

Ben with his breather in his mouth, and a job to do. He soon became an experienced diver, partly out of necessity. He's about to dive to free a snagged anchor below. Manihi lagoon, French Polynesia.

Touring the Andes with the Van Zwam family. We had fun exploring the Inca ruins and the cities of Quenca and Quito. The kids loved the outdoor marketplaces filled with all kinds of crafts, animals, and foods.

Shown is the *Emerald Jane*'s port stern, the only tiny section remaining after a long night. The mast sits directly behind it. (Photo courtesy of the French Navy)

The wreck of the *Emerald Jane* photographed at low tide the morning of our rescue. Below and to the left of the wreck is Ben's original reef camp. John lies in the red life raft to its right, surrounded by Jean and Amelia. (Photo courtesy of the French Navy)

The Taputo men crossing the lagoon to our rescue, having been alerted by the French Navy via a message in a bottle! They could get only so close in the larger boat, and then had to unload the smaller boat seen lying across its bows in order to cross the coral and shallows to bring us back out. (Photo courtesy of the French Navy)

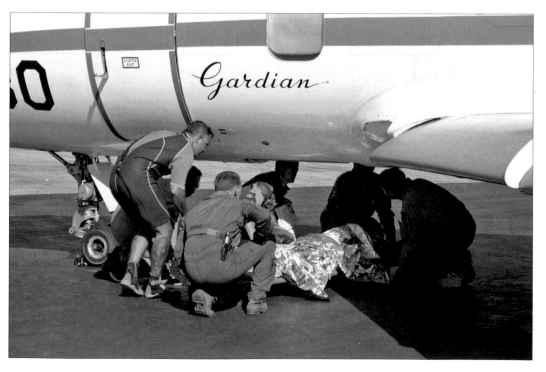

John, in the stretcher, couldn't fit through the door of the jet. The helicopter and jet crews are puzzling over how to load John through the bomb bay on the runway in Bora Bora in order to rush him to the hospital in Tahiti. (Photo courtesy of the French Navy)

Camille, looking haunted in the aftermath of the shipwreck, is given some comfort among the Taputo girls gathered around her in their hut above the lagoon, Scilly Atoll. (Photo courtesy of the French Army)

Diane and Papa Taputo, with the life raft that holds John seen in the background. Ben stands watch over him. (Photo courtesy of the French Army)

Leaving Tahiti-Faa'a International Airport for transport back to Los Angeles, with John's brother Mark and the Van Zwam family. We are all wearing the traditional Polynesian shell leis, given to us for a safe return trip by the helicopter and Gardian search plane rescue crews and their families, who so touchingly had come to the airport to wish us well. (Photo courtesy of the Van Zwam family)

(*Above*) John with the bronze award given to him by Vice Admiral Patrick Giaume, joined by the crews of the Puma helicopter, the Gardian aircraft, and support ground radio—to all of whom we owe our successful rescue. (Photo courtesy of the French Navy)

Dear Dad,
I love you very much and I envy you for how brave you are. I am very proud to have you as my father. You are my role model along with mom you are a great parent. There is no way to explain my love for you. I hope you get better soon!

Love,
your daughter
Amelia Silverwood

(*Left*) The get-well card Amelia made aboard *Fruity Fruits* and brought to her father's bedside the day after he arrived in the hospital in Papeete.

(*Above*) Captain Benjamin Franklin Pond of the *Julia Ann*, about 1856. (Courtesy of Meg Rasmussen)

(*Right*) Esther Spangenberg, passenger on the *Julia Ann*, about 1856. (Courtesy of Meg Rasmussen)

The Julia Ann *Entering San Francisco, 1852.* (Oil on canvas by David Thimgan, 1999, Australian National Maritime Museum Collection, USA Gallery. Reproduced courtesy of June Carey.)

Our family, together again, in La Jolla, California, August 2007. (© Michael Spengler)

While John and Ben were at the clinic, I took the kids to explore the beach. Out of my sight, Jack had started teasing a bull sea lion sunning his huge self on the beach. The sea lion soon got tired of this and lurched out in a lumbering waddle, grunting and snorting after Jack, who outran him, but was almost white with fright. New experience for Jack.

He was himself shortly, and was all over a giant tortoise.

"Jack," I warned, "don't get your fingers so near his mouth."

"It's a beak, Mom. Tortoises have beaks, same as birds."

The huge reptile—wide as a truck tire—blinked and slowly turned its face toward Jack, who held out a chunk of prickly pear fruit. When the tortoise slowly rose, extending its thick, scaly forelegs, Jack dropped the treat and ran again.

"He's a monster," he cried, but then he returned to study the creature's massive humped shell.

Even before leaving Ecuador, John and I sat down with the kids to read about the unique ecosystem of the Galápagos. Jack, of course, was the most enthusiastic, then and now, especially regarding the giant tortoises, which are among the largest and oldest reptiles in the world. Whalers used to keep them as livestock en route to Antarctica, and some were said to have weighed over a ton and must have been at least two hundred years old. John informed Jack that currently living in an Australian zoo is a tortoise that Charles Darwin personally carried aboard the HMS *Beagle.*

Amelia was fascinated by the marine iguanas that changed skin color from gray-green to black in order to absorb heat and regulate body temperature. Camille found the shuffling, dragonlike iguanas somewhat icky, so her favorite, she decided, were the flocks of colorful finches chirping in the thorny brush.

On our way back to the boat that afternoon, we could see that *Emerald Jane* had been commandeered by dozens of locals. Their glistening black bodies streamed overboard as we approached. Sea lions, they were, and every time we left the boat for an hour or more, they resumed their occupation. Ben chased the braver lions from the deck, who looked at us with contempt for not sharing this good sunning place.

That night aboard ship, nobody was interested in DVDs or computer games: Amelia had her sketchbook open on the dining table and was drawing a Galápagos tortoise munching a flower. Camille sat beside her, offering advice.

"Nose bigger," she said.

"Draw a bird on him," she added.

Jack was hitting the nature books.

Ben was at the chart table, studying winds and currents, and deciding that the surfing in the Marquesas would be pretty good. "Gnarly" was the word.

———

A week later, Steffan motored his dinghy slowly ahead of *Emerald Jane's* bow, guiding us through the twilight into the little reef-bound cove of Puerto Villamil, the only settlement on Isabela, a small island of the Galápagos. Clouds shrouded the volcanic caldera above the cove, accenting the island's primeval atmosphere. Ahead, we saw *Fruity Fruits* at anchor.

Once we were through the narrow harbor entrance, our view opened to large rocks covered with penguins and blue-footed boobies. Amelia was bouncing en pointe to see the small hopping penguins. The boobies, or at least their name, were the source of seemingly endless jokes for Camille and Jack. They have gray-flecked breast feathers, hooked beaks, and huge, neon-blue webbed feet. Their eyes are bright yellow and they wear a permanently startled expression. Galápagos penguins, less than eighteen inches high, dive and swim with the speed and grace of little dolphins.

We rode short-legged horses up through this paradise, up through the mist on a lava trail spilled from a volcano's caldera. Amelia stopped to collect tiny pieces of glassy lava for earrings. We entered a milky cloud. Vegetation became lush. Orchids were everywhere: gilded petals—amber and sapphire dangling from mossy branches.

The kids fell silent. It was too much beauty. There was nothing to say.

———

"Don't leave us, John," I whispered as I combed his bloody hair with my shaking fingers. I was leaning into the raft, feeling his temperature—so cold. He spit up a little as he chattered and tried to say he was okay. He looked at me. Amelia, who was keeping him warm, snuggled him and rubbed his exposed arm.

Amelia had always looked to John for leadership. The whole alcohol thing had shaken her. But, in a positive way, it had made her see him as a human being, like herself, like anyone, who got through the day with courage and character, not with some parental magic. She was learning all this just in time to lose him, it seemed. Even so, her kindness had always allowed her great moments with John, even in the worst of it. And he had always been so impressed with her. She could just do anything. She could sail a boat across the Pacific and cook up some brownies and bread at the same time. She was a ballerina. She was a good daughter for this man. I often watched her through the glass doors when she was at the wheel and I was doing something in the salon. She was something back there. No slouch.

Her perceptions and reports were so professional: "We've been averaging about 260 degrees, Dad, and our speed has been pretty steady around 7.5 knots." She reported this to John as we left the Galápagos and began the 3,300-mile first leg of our journey across the wide Pacific to Polynesia. She had started out the voyage with a cooking spree, and the smell of bread was twirling up into the sails.

Ben was another matter. He had been hoping the Pacific thing would maybe turn out to be a quick trip up Mexico to California and home. But he just didn't have the votes. When he heard with a certainty that we were going to be at sea beyond the summer months, and that he would be away from his social life for a good while longer, he locked his stateroom door and went into a funk. I was more worried than John; it wasn't quite like Ben to do this, and he wouldn't respond when we knocked and called—or when we then pounded and yelled. *Maybe he's not okay,* I thought. *Maybe he's sick and unconscious.*

Ben had just turned fifteen, and this moment was his last big good-bye to childhood. John crammed a screwdriver into the mahogany door frame and jimmied it open. Inside, Ben stared at us defiantly. Then he just broke down.

"I miss my friends. I miss them so much—this isn't fair."

John sat on the edge of the bunk and wrapped an arm around him. "Hey, pal," he said.

Ben missed his friends. He missed surfing. He desperately missed online computer games—which, like surfing, had made him feel competent. In big ports like Panama City he had been able to find Internet cafés with the necessary firepower for his games, but that wasn't going to happen in the little Pacific backwater ports ahead.

John reminded him that some of the best surfing in the world is in Tahiti. Didn't help much, as no one he cared about would be there to share it.

Amelia's banana bread and some quiet time eventually brought him back.

He was right—it was unfair. But to not have this experience? Maybe that would be unfair, too. So he let the wind blow its own way; it was not heading to California.

Ben caught a big fish the next day, which also helped. The boat was cranking along at over eight knots, which makes it hard to reel in a big one. John slacked the main to slow us down.

Ben's fish broke from the water, a bullet-shaped beauty with a rainbow shimmer. It jumped again, trying to shake loose, but Ben kept the line taut—we had a twenty-pound mahimahi for dinner that night and the next, with fish tacos for lunch. He was the big provider, and that made him settle into the trip. He began teaching his little brother how to tie fishing lures and, remarkably, he stopped calling him a moron whenever Jack didn't quite get something. Jack, in turn, stopped calling Ben a big jerk. The Seven Years' War had run its course. They would catch skipjack and mahimahi, and one afternoon in the middle of the Pacific they would battle and wonder what monster snapped their eighty-pound fishing line.

These were long miles and long weeks of sailing alone under the vast blue bowl of the Pacific sky. We all got closer. Amelia read to Camille and carried her into the salon for her nap. Some mornings they played dress-up and dabbled with lipstick and blush. She helped Camille do her preschool workbooks.

For myself, I took the calm of early mornings to write our log, compose and answer e-mails, and listen to the sea lapping under the boat. I got bread and breakfast going. One by one, the kids would roll out of their bunks and poke around the charts and the instruments before helping with breakfast.

When Ben got tired of watching the same James Bond DVDs, he started actually reading. He read Tom Clancy thrillers and got completely hooked—always had his nose in a book. He would describe the stories in excruciating detail to his father, and John would eat it up.

"Okay, Dad, so this guy, the Russian . . ."

Amelia worked every day with her paints and pastels. She was getting very good

John often joined Camille and Jack on the salon floor, building elaborate Lego cities and seaports. Speedy the tortoise roamed these streets like Godzilla.

We ate together around the cockpit table. I would always put Camille to bed, reading her to sleep in my arms.

Because things can't be left around in the confined space of a boat, the kids had learned to put away things, clean things, wash dishes as soon as they were used. I watched and wondered if it would stick. But nothing lasts forever; enjoy it now, I told myself.

The crossing was not without crisis and danger: A line broke and two thousand square feet of sail blew into the sea, where we ran over it and it fouled in the propeller shafts. John had to go under the boat with a knife and figure it out. He was gone a long time between breaths, but he had Ben to help him, and it all got sorted out. The ocean floor was three dark miles below.

The stars and planets were brilliant: Mars was as red as a flare; Venus and Jupiter made the waves glitter. The Milky Way arched from horizon to horizon. John and the boat and the sky and the ocean really became one as he steered late at night.

At 2:00 a.m. he would wake Jack with a whiff of the Panama chocolate, and they would sail together. Three whiffs and Jack would be on his feet, stumbling back to the starboard deck for a private, late-night pee into the sea. He had a thing about that, and I guess we sort of gave up after a while.

Little Jack just liked peeing over the edge. Years earlier, I had the worst time potty-training him. A friend suggested I teach him to pee outside, as boys love to do that, she said. Worked like a charm. It worked too well. Jack is an enthusiastic creature and once he finds something cool he is all over it. We were at a party for the opening of John's model homes, and John and I were talking to a group of potential buyers who suddenly were looking beyond us to the little guy watering the beautiful flowers.

John and I, of course, had a porthole in our cabin, as did all the staterooms. Ours was different in that, many early mornings, there was a little special rain outside—God forbid a breeze. We scolded and punished and asked him please to use the head right next to his stateroom, or at least the stern of the boat. But he is a free soul.

Once when we were anchored right across from $1,000-per-night stilt huts in Bora-Bora, a Japanese honeymoon couple, out on their morning deck, ran inside to spare themselves the sight of Jack recycling his water. We were asked to move. Jack complained that it was perfectly natural—every animal does it—but he would try to remember to use the head. However, in the dark of midocean, with just two men awake, well, Jack would save another bit of wear and tear on the toilet pump.

After his ceremony, he would go back to the wheel with his father to learn about the stars, about the different kinds and sizes of waves, about how to write in the log, even how to plot our position on the map from the numbers on the GPS display in the cockpit, above the salon door.

Before dawn on the last day crossing the Pacific, I wrote up the log and plotted our position. At eight knots we should reach Hiva Oa, our planned landfall in the Marquesas Islands, before noon. Depending on the weather, our first sight of land after sixteen days at sea should be Temetiu, the axe-blade volcanic ridge that rises to almost four thousand feet. We were all very excited to be completing the long passage.

Hiva Oa is a volcanic mountain that erupted from the floor of the South Pacific less than three million years ago—a mere moment in geologic time. The island's Polynesian name means "main roof beam," as it was thought by the ancients to support the sky.

Out in the cockpit, I peered ahead beneath the bulging genoa. There was distant lightning, probably from the high peak of the still-invisible monolith ahead.

I had been a little apprehensive about this long, lonely stretch of sea, but now I was thinking I would miss the peacefulness of our isolation. We had run sixteen days all alone.

Then, with the dawn, I saw it in the distance: Hiva Oa, the Marquesas. We had done it.

We cruised quietly into a small harbor below green-as-Ireland ridges. Above them, mist hung on jagged peaks—we could see a waterfall. We would soon be climbing through the island's jungles, finding the ancient altars and the frightening stone tiki heads where a human price had often been paid to keep the volcano happy.

We hiked to the grave of artist Paul Gauguin. In the small town below, Amelia bought prints of his paintings of the island.

"Look at the *colors*," she said, feeling the paper like found gold. "And the people! They're not realistic, but they *are* so real." In that instant, she had learned the genius of Post-Impressionism. When we arrived in Tahiti, she would buy fabrics with the bold colors and designs she had seen first through Gauguin's eyes.

I can picture John up at Gauguin's grave site, telling the kids about this artist with vision, who had a dream that wouldn't be denied, who came halfway across the world to drink in this beauty. The *Emerald Jane* was far below us in a beautiful anchorage. Amelia and Ben smiled at their father, completely getting it—getting him.

Ben finally got to surf in some worthy waves. He had never seen waves like this. Neither had Jack, who lost his little board in an instant and had to be rescued by a French fellow, very nice-looking.

Fine-looking people were popping up all over, as the *Fruity Fruits* sailed in behind us, and we resumed our friendship. Ben regaled their Jason with fishing and surfing stories. Amelia showed Stephanie the clothes she'd sewn. Carolyne and I shared some champagne when the men were out; we had a custom of christening each new port.

My fears about alcohol had softened, mainly because John was now up front with people about the fact that he was an alcoholic, unable to drink with us. That had happened with the help of a sailing couple we met in Ecuador. They were both very frank about their alcoholism: "No thanks, I don't drink—can't handle the stuff." Almost like a food allergy. This was somehow a huge moment for me. It's just a thing you don't do if your body can't handle it.

After a few weeks, we headed for Tahiti by way of Manihi, one of the large atolls in the remote Tuamotus—a three-day sail. We anchored in a lagoon known for its black pearls. It was a calm anchorage, allowing John to go to the top of our eighty-foot sail to fix a frayed line. Ben hoisted him up by cranking a pulley line from the deck. Up there, John could look down to the tiny boat surrounded by the azure lagoon. Amelia and Camille were dancing and singing on the sandy shore, as they so often did. Hundreds of baby reef sharks were swirling around Jack, who was sidestroking back to the boat, holding a three-foot octopus.

It was my birthday. John asked me what I wanted and I reminded him of the black pearls below us. He went down there and I thought, well, if he finds one, it will say something about our future as a couple. He could not find one. That was all right. Just a thought.

The days and islands ahead were for snorkling, diving, hiking, and horseback riding, and beach runs for me. Schoolwork was over for the year. The kids were improving their scuba diving skills and seeing everything underwater—Amelia was so amazed to see an eight-foot-wide manta ray flapping along the bottom of a lagoon, to see so many colors and designs down there.

Humpback whales seemed to be guiding us through the fog the Sunday morning we sailed into Tahiti.

Shore leave in Papeete, Tahiti, offered all the French Polynesian foods and entertainments that people dream. Ukulele rhythms and war chants filled the streets around the harbor.

The generator, bought new in Panama, went out. Replacement parts were six weeks away. We had to move the boat to where a crane could pull the generator. The U.S. manufacturer argued over the phone about the warranty. Was it installed properly? Did water get into it? The local dealer said it was installed properly and had not gotten wet. But the company wanted to see the parts, please. So we were high and dry for a month and a half on a very expensive island. It changed our plans; we wanted to get to Australia before the cyclone season.

So, you say to yourself, that's how the wind is blowing today. Take a breath. Look at the view. Later that same day, I watched a sunset of remarkable beauty from the deck of *Emerald Jane.* In the distance, like Bali

Ha'i, was the island of Moorea floating in red and gold. My ability to look for the silver lining was tested a few minutes later when Camille came running down the dock: Jack had crashed his skateboard and broken his arm. Yes, he had his helmet: He put it down in a safe place before he started skating.

I had resisted a skateboard for how many thousand miles? He had kept up the pressure. So many other kids along the docks were having so much fun. And he had been pretty good at it back home on Ben's board. When he and I saw a very good board at half-price in a market, I gave in.

So, I was not feeling like the good mom now. I called someone we knew on the island, Emily, a middle-aged Tahitian woman. She ran to the boat, so pretty in her flowing Tahitian dress. She has a beautiful, happy face and wears her long, black hair in a bun. I called her because she is a taxi driver and would know the best place to go and could translate when we got there. She loaded us into the back of her taxi and sped us to the "best hospital in Polynesia."

Jack was in miserable pain. An emergency room doctor clamped a laughing-gas mask to his nose.

"Be nice," Jack said through the mask, "or I'm calling my lawyer."

The smiling doctor turned on the gas.

Emily's husband, a tall, thin American who wears his hair long but is balding and gray, and who wears shorts, sneakers, and a Polynesian shirt, rushed John to the hospital from another direction. He told John that the hospital was without a doubt the very worst in Polynesia. As for his own health, he had seen a vision of the Virgin Mary recently and hadn't been sick a day since.

The hospital did a fine job.

———

Waiting for parts, we explored the white sands and turquoise lagoons of Moorea, Huahini, the twin islands of Raiatea and Tahaa, and Bora-Bora. Dormant volcanoes were draped in clouds and rain forests. Jack was on the hunt for hermit crabs and Ben would jump off the stern each morning with his surfboard, finding local boys to surf with for the day.

Docked in yacht harbors reminds one just how much bloody money there is in the world. In Tahiti's harbors, you will find people more like us—people who have worked hard and saved up for the adventure. But often, especially in the Caribbean, you will see the very rich. We found ourselves in marina slips beside people of remarkable means. Yes, the Van Z's were not poor, but you can meet many South African businesspeople with big boats because the government of South Africa does not allow people to move money out of the country. People buy expensive boats and they sail their money out in the form of canvas, brass, and mahogany. It's a strategy more than a lifestyle, though it may easily become that.

Quite beyond that sort of thing, some of the boats next to us belonged to the world's truly rich. Back in Aruba, we docked next to a 150-foot motor yacht with a twelve-member professional crew. Ben dared to ask the owner, a New Jersey man, what it cost to keep afloat. A million dollars a year was the answer given as he left the dock to go buy cashmere sweaters for everyone—the air-conditioning on the brand-new boat was too cold. We saw many yachts of that size during our travels, some with dinghies the size of small yachts, and some even with helicopters.

We were docked in Tahiti directly across from Le Retro, a popular French café. Next to us was a beautiful British yacht with two occupants: the thirtysomething captain, Andy, and the owner, a fortysomething woman entrepreneur from London. We had met them before, in the Marquesas. Their yacht was a sleek, racy "True Love" sailing ship. The woman was fair-skinned and pretty with short dark hair, about average height. I admired her style greatly—she was one of those determined women who gets what she wants and has fun doing it. Her dream was to sail around the world, so she bought a big boat and hired a movie-star-tan captain. Not bad.

The two seemed very close, and we assumed they were married or at least a couple. Andy said matter-of-factly to John, when questioned, "Oh no, I work for her. I am her captain." Well, yes.

One very hot Saturday afternoon, there was a street protest right off the harbor. Tahitians were walking with signs and driving in cars and pickup trucks to protest French president Jacques Chirac's desire to reappoint the current French president of Tahiti for another term. The people wanted an election—they wanted to elect a Polynesian. After the gentle protest went by, and after I watched an old man fishing off the dock and tossing firecrackers into the water to attract the fish—it certainly did not work—I noticed a Polynesian man going belowdecks on the British yacht beside us. I hadn't seen him before. The woman was off wakeboarding, so I wondered what was up. Maybe the captain and the lady were indeed not a couple. Maybe he had other interests.

That was not the case. Captain Andy was just getting out of the shower when he saw this man taking his camera and wallet from his stateroom. Andy tied on his bath towel, and the two men came exploding up the companionway to the deck, then across to the dock and out to the street.

They ran up a narrow side alley to a park, knocking down people who were shopping and participating in the protest. Andy lost his towel but kept after the man, with the crowd cheering on this great race. Andy caught him and tackled him to the ground. He got his camera and wallet back, then walked back for his towel, which bystanders tossed to him with some applause.

"Bravo!" we said as he stood near the stern of *Emerald Jane* in his towel to give us the full accounting.

"Well, yes, sorry," he said, looking down at himself, "bit of a chase around town. This chap came aboard and tried to pinch my things."

"Really!" I said, "Pinch your things!"

We of course invited him aboard, and he paced around beautifully as he recounted every cut and turn of the chase. He and the owner have become our good friends.

I wake up the next morning at 5:00, lying in bed with nervous adrenaline running through my system—not unusual for me. I didn't know what it was; my thoughts ran frantically from one worry to another. Everything suddenly seemed like a major problem, especially myself. *Why am I such a bad wife and mother? My kids are so unhappy: They complain about their schoolwork, the boredom, and their too-distant friends. They want to go back to California. They want to go see a movie in English. They want to eat American food. John is happy for the most part, but he has to listen to my fretting constantly.* I tried to go back to sleep or get up, but I am pinned down by my worries. *Ben is getting fat. I tell him every day he can't eat all the food he wants. He won't exercise. "Ben, go for a walk, run, swim—stop eating those chow mein sandwiches." Tahitians make chow mein sandwiches on French baguettes, and they gave the first one free to Ben. I'm on Ben's case all the time now.*

And Jack! Jack procrastinates on his schoolwork. I have to sit at the table with him again today and probably get angry with him. We will be stuck here in French Polynesia forever and will never get the generator fixed. We spent $10,000 for a new generator and now we have to lay out more money. John takes so long to fix things and if we want it done faster he has to hire someone, and it costs too much and I think they are ripping us off. We can't even talk to them in English. Thank God for Laurant, our boat-repair agent—at least he speaks English, but we have to pay him, too. Steffan fixes everything himself. Will we have enough money to go home to? So much money has been thrown into this boat—we will never recoup it when we sell her. I can't do a thing about it. We can't just pack everything up and go home.

I finally go and write in my journal about how I am feeling and what happened the day before. It helps put things in perspective. *Today it's extra difficult to relax and write: I feel as though I'm going to jump out of my skin when the slightest thing goes wrong. I will blow like a volcano. I am verbally abusive to John and the kids. Snippy remarks and sarcasm. They give me a wide berth. I spend a lot of time with Camille, at Jack's expense—Amelia takes up the slack. I pay special attention to Camille. She snuggles each night in the cabin with me, works on her homework, and loves everything. Never is a problem.*

After this anxiety comes some depression. I will have coffee out in the cockpit and try to concentrate on the beauty.

Oh, and I will have to go into an Internet café today and pay all the bills. And I need to finish our tax return.

At 6:30, Carolyne is standing on the dock waiting for me. If we were at anchor, I would pick her up in the dinghy or she would pick me up, but today we are lucky to be able to just step off the boat and hit the pavement.

We run past the cruise and ferry terminals. We take in the air and taste the salt and the auto exhaust. The air is balmy already. We proceed over the bridge by the marine store. The fumes fade now and only the smell of the Pacific Ocean remains. The sun is rising and the sky absolutely fills with colors.

Carolyne has the same kinds of feelings sometimes, so she knows and listens. She gives me advice on how to handle the kids and John. Her own kids were driving her crazy yesterday.

As my body begins to really sweat, the anxiety and depression lift. What the hell—it's going to be a fine day. Things work out. Enough things will be said to make us laugh as we run. Damn fine run. I hated— really, truly hated—to say goodbye to her not long after that.

You can only stay in paradise so long without having to leave for a time and come back with a renewed visa. I suppose it keeps the beach-combers from settling in—they at least have to have the wherewithal to travel away and travel back. Still waiting for repairs, we flew to New Zealand to explore its breathtaking mountains, valleys, and coasts for three weeks in a rented camper van.

I had to do the driving. New Zealanders drive on the left side of the road, therefore the stick shift is to the left of the wheel. The mountain roads were steep and narrow in many places, so it wasn't a great place to learn how to drive all over again.

The reason I had to drive was that John sometimes gets lost in his own thoughts at a million miles an hour and will tune you out. He tuned out people back in Ecuador who told us never to keep a wallet in a back pocket. Moments later, after a slight crush of the market crowd, John was without wallet, cash, credit cards, and driver's license. We canceled the cards and eventually got replacements, but the driver's license was still a problem. So I drove because he sometimes doesn't pay attention. It's part of his charm, you could say.

I did hit something: The high camper top tore against a low part of a building. But I am the planner and the worrier, so we had full rental insurance.

John didn't mind having a driver. He could look at the scenery all the better. He waved, chatted at every stop; I think he had decided to get to know every human being in New Zealand. Also, John is a business guy at heart and he was seeing opportunities for property development. People were introducing him to other people. He couldn't go to an AA meeting without coming back with a pocket full of cards. Part of his success as a developer in California was that I was standing behind him with organizing skills—not his strong suit. And our home was California, not New Zealand. It was a worry. It was a worry that he was thinking of spending enough time there after the voyage to do business, which would be a kind of separation. And a business risk.

After New Zealand, we flew back to Tahiti. Then, amazingly, we flew back to California to check on things and let the weather clear in the South Pacific while the repairs were completed. Being back in the United States felt great. The kids rushed to connect with their pals, but many of them had moved on to other friends. When it was time to return and complete the voyage, almost everyone was ready to do that. We had missed our life on the *Emerald Jane.* I say almost everyone because Ben really wanted to stay. He had found friends in the islands, surfing, paintball wars, just hanging out, but his old friends were his real friends.

He got his learner's driving permit while we were back. He wasn't supposed to drive by himself, but the day before we were to fly back to Tahiti he was gone in our old Jeep. I decided not to worry about it. He sped into the driveway late in the evening, not talking to anyone. He packed and silently headed to the airport with us, red hot inside.

Before we left, I told John to look around: There were still plenty of opportunities in California for him—for us.

Yes, but . . . He had been here and done this. He is so hungry for the new. He had seen something there. "I'm not serious about it," he told me on the plane back to Tahiti. "It's just something to consider. We'll see. When I'm getting the boat cleaned up and sold in Sydney, maybe I can take another recon trip over there."

He was going to do this thing. I could feel it.

He was going to do it, just as Ben had insisted on bungee jumping into a canyon in New Zealand. Leaps of faith run in the family.

Odd the things you worry about when you are hanging around a coral reef and you should be worried about more immediate things. Well, there was not going to be a boat to fix up and sell in Australia. Maybe we needed this reef somehow. High price to pay. High price. I kept reaching into the raft to stroke John's head, his neck, feel his skin, make sure he was alive.

AN EXPLOSION

An explosion came from the direction of the ledge camp. I turned quickly to see what mishap had now befallen my family. It was nothing like that. Ben was standing on the high coral like a victorious soldier on a hilltop. He held a flare tube in his still-upstretched hand. The flare he had just launched was now a beautiful crimson firework in the morning sky. Then I heard what he had heard: an airplane. A low-flying French Navy jet.

Little Jack was jumping next to Ben, honest-to-God shouting, "The plane! The plane!" Camille was struggling to her feet beside the boys. They were waving like crazy.

"My God," I shouted into the canopy of the life raft, "They found us." John's eyes opened and his lips, always moving slightly with prayer, stopped and opened slightly. He looked into my eyes.

Ben fired another flare, which made me jump like the first one.

The jet screamed low over us.

"Is he circling?" John struggled to say.

I didn't answer; I started yelling and waving with the kids. Why would someone yell at a jet? Well, how are you going to not do that? We yelled magnificently. Our exhausted, tired, lacerated, thirsty bodies jumped around like cheerleaders.

The jet banked in the distance and roared over us again, tipping its wings in salute. As it came yet again, I gathered everyone around the life raft and we pointed into it, hoping they would understand.

"Listen to that, Dad!" Ben shouted. "They're right above us, Dad! We're gonna get you out of here!"

The jet circled again and then flew off to the northeast. I saw it fly low over a line of distant palm trees that had, until now, been invisible in the glare of the sunrise; the coral atoll island was near or maybe even attached to a *motu:* a small island. The jet seemed to mess around over by the palms, and then it returned to buzz low over us. Then it was gone.

———

Things had been happening beyond our view; the little beacon in Jack's embrace had finally pointed in the right direction at the right moment as a satellite passed. Despite my dark fears that maybe, like our first satellite phone, the beacon didn't work in the Pacific at all; it did.

Petty Officer Kevin Denicker was the U.S. Coast Guard's Search and Rescue Duty Officer on call in Alameda, California, when the first distress call from *Emerald Jane's* emergency beacon arrived via satellite. He assigned the message "emergency" status and quickly read the encoded information contained in the beacon's identification data: *Emerald Jane*, sailboat, homeport San Diego, emergency family phone numbers in New York and Pennsylvania.

The signal had been picked up in New Zealand, so he checked available search-and-rescue assets in the South Pacific. At first, that general area was the only location known, because our beacon's GPS coordinates had not come through as part of the signal. All unlocated beacons throughout the entire Pacific become Alameda's responsibility, and Denicker could have shelved the problem until better information arrived, but he did not. He e-mailed and faxed all the information he had to Coast Guard Station, San Diego, asking them to initiate checks for boats matching *Emerald Jane*'s description with local marinas and the San Diego Harbor Master, in the event that the distress call was a false alarm from a boat safely home—over 70 percent of beacon alarms are exactly that. Seven minutes after the distress call arrived, the Coast Guard was tracking down our families to see if they knew our sailing course. The lights were just then flickering out on the *Emerald Jane*.

It was after midnight in Pleasantville, Westchester County, New York, when my father answered the call from the Coast Guard. He told them we were en route to Australia, which was correct—it was our eventual destination. Coast Guard San Diego then called the *Emerald Jane*'s iridium satellite phone, but it was already underwater in a flooded cabin. It was 7:33 p.m. on the reef. At that moment, our boat flexed into the reef and *Emerald Jane*'s mast came crashing down.

Coast Guard Station San Diego next tried e-mailing *Emerald Jane* over its Global Marine Services account, but to no avail. Denicker, after talking to our family, now believed Bora-Bora was our likely starting point. We were probably between there and Australia.

He phoned the RCC Australia and New Zealand, recognizing the impossible immensity of the search area but wanting to get them on board. He also wanted New Zealand to contact their closest search-and-rescue area to the east, the French Polynesian Tahiti search-and-rescue region.

Denicker telephoned RCC New Zealand and requested they also contact the French government's search-and-rescue center in Papeete. The French reported that "bad storms at sea" had passed through the area. The New Zealand officials asked the French to consult their people in Bora-Bora and remain in contact.

At 8:16 p.m. Central Pacific Time, a low-earth orbit satellite with a rescue beacon receiver aboard crossed above the South Pacific. It failed to detect the distress signal of *Emerald Jane,* possibly due to atmospheric interference.

It was 8:34 p.m., more than ninety minutes after that first distress call had gone out, when a third satellite swept over the Pacific horizon from the south. This was a NOAA weather satellite, also carrying a search-and-rescue module. At an apogee of 528 miles, the satellite was approaching the closest it would ever be to the wreck of *Emerald Jane.* This was a Cadillac of satellites, weighing more than five thousand pounds at launch, six feet wide and fourteen feet long, plus a solar power array of nine by twenty feet. It was a weather and environmental monitoring satellite in a polar orbit.

It captured two ambiguously "split" GPS positions for *Emerald Jane* and relayed those positions to the Earth station in Bundaberg, Queensland, Australia. From there, the coordinates were instantly relayed through Australian Mission Control Center in Canberra to Alameda, California, and simultaneously to French Mission Control in Toulouse, in the South of France.

The ambiguous position data left Kevin Denicker with a search box bounded on the west by Australia's Gold Coast, east 3,000 miles to Bora-Bora, and 700 miles from north to south. That meant an impossibly large search area of 2,100,000 square miles.

My father, Albert Boera, called San Diego back at 1:40 a.m. Eastern. He now remembered my telling him that the boat was leaving from Raiatea, Tahiti, not Bora-Bora, and that the earliest *Emerald Jane* could have sailed was June 21. He had also recalled that we would be stopping in Tonga before going on to Australia.

The conversation was immediately relayed to Alameda, where Denicker reasoned the *Emerald Jane* could only have been at sea four days at the most, having sailed a maximum of 800 miles toward Tonga, about 1,400 miles from Raiatea. This argued for a smaller search box, and one closer to Polynesia than Australia. The smaller box still contained a quarter-million square miles, but it was getting smaller.

At 8:40 p.m. Central Pacific, the angle of the tiny emergency radio beacon's antenna aligned exactly for a brief moment with the GOES-10 satellite over the equator. Through some quirk of atmospherics, GOES-10 picked up the weak signal at a distance of 25,000 miles and retransmitted down to Wellington, New Zealand, with a single set of coordinates. In the dry terminology of the rescue business, an "AMBIGUITY RESOLVED TO THE FOLLOWING POSITION" message simultaneously appeared on console screens in New Zealand, Australia, California, and France. *Emerald Jane*'s location coordinates were now known to within a few yards: It was hard aground on the semisubmerged reef of Scilly Island.

Denicker consulted the Department of Defense's Global Command and Control System to determine the position of any U.S. Navy vessels close enough to help *Emerald Jane*. There were none. From a voluntary computerized system enabling ships at sea worldwide to assist in high-seas rescues, Denicker learned there were no ships within 300 miles of *Emerald Jane*—the closest was fifteen hours away. He nevertheless received a welcome fax from RCC New Zealand stating that the French had a Navy vessel on its way.

Unfortunately, this was an erroneous report, common in situations involving quick action by many governments and in many languages.

The French RCC Tahiti informed Alameda, by way of Hawaii, that they were attempting to contact *Emerald Jane*. If they could not, they would have a search plane in the air that night and a boat on its way in the morning.

At the Papeete Rescue Coordination Center, French Navy officers tried calling our iridium satellite phone. Then they tried reaching us by high-frequency radio—getting nothing, of course.

There is a tiny settlement on Scilly, home to a single Polynesian family—the Taputus—but the family would not be monitoring the inter-island radio until 5:00 a.m.

Coast Guard Headquarters Hawaii checked in with Denicker to let him know that the French had just announced they were not, in fact, putting a plane in the air that night; it was against policy. The search aircraft would depart Papeete at first light, 6:00 a.m. They would make a decision on the need for a rescue boat later.

The Tahiti RCC alerted the on-call crew of the French Navy's 25F L'Escadron de Transport d'Outre-Mer, the local search-and-rescue unit based at Tahiti. This crew flies the Dassault twin-jet Gardian, a long-range patrol aircraft.

The RCC reached aircraft commander Capitaine de Corvette Eric Mahoudo at his home in Papeete a little after 11:30 p.m. The Gardian would fly reconnaissance to Scilly, arriving just after dawn. If wreckage were seen, a French Air Force Super Puma helicopter with a skilled paramedic rescue crew and a doctor would be dispatched.

The Tahiti RCC then called the commander of the Super Puma rescue helicopter, Captaine Sebastien Roger, ordering him to put his crew on standby. Roger's maximum flight range was between 350 and 400 nautical miles, depending on the winds aloft. The flying distance between Tahiti and Scilly Island was 350 miles.

Denicker waited to hear that the search jet had taken off. He had never been able to get them on the radio or telephone directly, and more and more messages seemed contradictory.

He immediately issued a high-frequency radio Marine Alert satellite text broadcast to all vessels, public and private, in the Pacific Ocean: "A Marine Alert has been issued by RCC Alameda for mariners in the vicinity of 16 degrees, 35 minutes, 3 seconds South, and 154 degrees, 42 minutes, 1 second West. Any mariners transiting the area please be on the lookout ... Render all possible assistance ..."

Almost six hours had passed since *Emerald Jane*'s original distress call. RCC Papeete called Denicker to ask how many persons were likely on board. They said they hoped to use native fisherman nearby to assist in the rescue.

Ernie Delli Gatti, a twenty-nine-year veteran of Air Force search-and-rescue operations, came on duty in Alameda and was briefed by Denicker at 7:00 a.m. Delli Gatti called RCC Papeete and insisted that a jet be made ready to take off the minute it was needed to move any injured to a trauma hospital. He contacted the American consular agent in Tahiti, Christopher Kozely, and put him on standby to help with any bureaucratic or logistical issues.

Aircraft commander Eric Mahoudo sat in the left cockpit seat of the Dassault Gardian TO80. Beside him, copilot Lieutenant Olivier Eynard completed the last of the instrument checks. The amber lights of Tahiti-Faa'a International Airport stretched toward the dark dawn horizon. It was 5:21 a.m. Tahiti time, Sunday, June 26, 2005.

"Prêt à décoller…" Ready for takeoff.

As a prayer service for our family was beginning in faraway California, Mahoudo throttled forward.

While our friends prayed, the Gardian aircraft was lifting off, bound for the little atoll island of Scilly.

At 6:10 a.m., radar operator Daniel Raingeval had the island on his scope. Radio operator Michel Blanchard and flight mechanic Vincent Desmidt took up stations at the large windows on either side of the plane. Mahoudo eased the throttles and began a long power glide toward the island.

In French nautical terms, the reef was a "platier," a dangerously low-lying coral shelf usually submerged.

Mahoudo brought the Gardian in on a curving bank, 1,200 feet above the reef.

They had a red flare in sight from the reef, where white wreckage was now visible, littered like a plane crash along the reef. And then another flare. Ben was firing the red missiles into the sky.

The jet circled twice more and then flew away, low and slow toward the family huts across the lagoon. Mahoudo radioed Tahiti and recommended launching the Super Puma helicopter to pick up the survivors.

Captain Mahoudo roared low over the rusty roofs of the tiny island's only inhabitants, the Taputu family and their fourteen children. They lived off the sea, a garden, and the coconut palms. The family jumped down from their stilt houses and ran to a nearby clearing. Through the plane's flare tube, flight mechanic Vincent Desmidt dropped a plastic Orangina bottle with a message inside: Would they please render assistance to some Americans across the lagoon until a helicopter could come? *Merci.* The bottle fluttered into the lagoon and the Taputu children jumped in to retrieve it. The plane passed over again as Mr. Taputu read the message and waved up to them. *Oui, oui,* pointing across the lagoon; he understood. His boys were already pulling the boat down to the water. The jet would guide them across the great expanse of the heart-shaped lagoon to the farside reef.

The jet dropped a rescue flare into the lagoon near us, and it streaked a thick orange smoke across the sky. I held open the torn entrance door of the raft's canopy so that John could see it, and so the sun could flood in and warm him. He moaned so weakly now, shivered so weakly.

Ben resumed his review of our debris. He found a small plastic box of his contact lenses, a great prize. He shouted the news to me and held them up.

I walked toward Ben. There was debris everywhere. I found a tennis racket, the cockpit refrigerator, a surfboard. Suddenly I spotted a clear plastic bottle of Vicodin painkiller that I had purchased in the pharmacy two long years ago in California. It was sticking upright in a small crevice unharmed and dry. It seemed almost as if an angel had placed it their for me to find. I took the bottle back and gave John two pills with a sip of cola. It took him awhile to swallow and he vomited shortly after. I doubt that it helped ease the pain, but perhaps it gave him a boost.

I looked out toward the ocean and my eyes focused on the crushed and splintered white shell of *Emerald Jane*. I stood there staring for a long time and felt a sagging pain deep in my throat. I remembered all the endless repairs and maintenance delays, my anguish over the money flowing out for equipment, but none of that seemed to matter. *Emerald Jane* had become a part of the family, and now she was gone.

After several hours, and now coming directly through the bright sun, a boatful of Polynesian men waved to us. They paddled their craft toward the coral ledge. They smiled broadly. "Is this a dream? What type of rescue is this?"

"Ia Orana! Maita'i oe?" the eldest of them called out in Tahitian. Then he switched to French: "Bonjour, M'dame! Bonjour, les enfants!"

They were of this reef and they greeted us, welcomed us, took care of us for a time as their own.

———

John was barely alive when the helicopter arrived in a clearing near the home of the Taputus, where that family had so graciously cared for us. They gave us clothes and food. When Diane Taputu realized that we were truly in shock, she gave Camille the gold-and-black-pearl bracelet off her wrist. Camille smiled for the first time since the accident. Diane turned and took off the necklace from her husband's neck—an ornate gold tiki holding a large black pearl—and put it on Amelia, who smiled and cried a little and hugged her. Then Diane lifted off her own gold-and-black-pearl necklace and put it on me. I protested that we couldn't accept these gifts, but Diane Taputu only smiled and shook her head and held me.

"They are a gift from our family to our new friends," she whispered in the smooth French of Tahiti. I could understand enough to grasp what she was saying. I did not argue. This was the pearl I had wanted as a good luck charm for our marriage. How amazing that it should have come in this moment!

I counted fourteen children. "Tous sont les vôtres?" I asked. Yes, all hers and her husband's. Her eyes said she was extremely proud of her family. Indeed, they all looked very happy, even with the little they had. Or did they have it all?

Maybe there was one thing they didn't have: I asked if I could use their bathroom. She snickered and led me to tiny, doorless hut. A toilet was placed over a hole in the sand. The family chickens followed me inside to see what the new folks were like.

French Navy medics saved John's life on the long lift to the first hospital and took him by jet to the next.

He lost his leg, of course, and we didn't care the least about that, compared with having him alive. Actually, Jack, who is our biologist, thought it was a shame to just throw the leg away, but he was unsuccessful in getting it back from the surgeons.

After undertaking a second surgery to take more of his leg above the knee, and then after three weeks in a hospital upon returning to California, he went through a hard period of adjustment and rehabilitation.

John is fine with his new leg, which has enough electronics in it to keep him happy. For me, returning home and being the caregiver never seemed to end, but it did. I recovered with therapy and learning the practice of Primordial sound meditation—I had been getting some panic attacks out of the blue.

The kids did very well back in school. Amelia came back different from some of her friends. For one thing, she really could no longer see the need to buy expensive designer clothes. She was soon down in Mexico with a teen volunteer program that helps build homes for the very poor. Some of her pals were talking on the way down about the expensive purses they were going to get for presents. Once there, some didn't know how to use a paintbrush or a broom. Some were hanging out in the bus on their cell phones instead of helping, demanding that the driver please leave on the air-conditioning. She said she almost had to laugh; they are her friends, as always, but she can now "see outside the box they're in." That is what she said.

Would she take her own family on a trip like that someday? Yes, she says. Yes, say Jack and Camille, jumping up. Ben says he would too, but by land.

Soon after our return, Ben received the Boy Scout's highest award for valor: The Honor Medal with Crossed Palms. It is awarded for unusual heroism and for extraordinary skill or resourcefulness in saving a life at extreme risk to oneself. Most of the lifesaving skills that he used on the reef were, in fact, skills he learned in Scouts.

He was soon after accepted at Annapolis, his dream school. Then, out of nowhere, a letter came reneging the acceptance after a review of his eyesight. I thought it would crush him. He got over it and moved on.

He was accepted at Cal Poly as an engineering student, and he turned his excitment in that direction. The wind just wasn't blowing toward Annapolis, and he had learned to work with the wind. Those contact lenses he had found and held high from the wreckage were in a way a symbol of his freedom: His imperfect eyes would be perfect enough to show him a different direction—his own direction—to the future.

The beauty we found in the world was not only in the sea and the sky, but it was in the people we met everywhere, rich and poor, all colors. They received us so graciously and helped us whenever we needed help. They offered us everything in love, not as commerce. It is just a most beautiful planet in that way.

The people of the U.S. Coast Guard, the French Navy and other U.S. and French forces never let up for a second in their effort to find us and save us, just as the U.S. Coast Guard and friendly navies had protected us from pirates in the waters off Central and South America. We were so proud to meet them and will be forever thankful to them.

The big question, and I don't mind when friends ask: Was it worth it?

My friend Carolyne and I shared a bottle of champagne each time we reached a new port—just us, the whole bottle. My husband took me to secluded beaches—just us, the whole afternoon. My daughter and I raced each other on beautiful horses along the surf in Aruba and through the pineapple fields of Moorea, laughing so hard after. I saw my kids become interesting; I saw two of them grow up. The answer is yes.

BOOK II

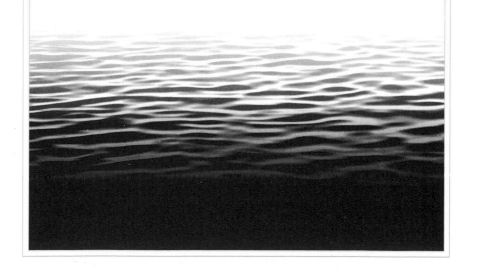

[1]

ANGELS

I didn't know how long I had been gone or where I was. Everything was blindingly white. I thought I was in some kind of barbershop, and the sheet tucked around me was to catch my hair. An angel of some sort— she was nurse Pascale but I thought she might be an angel—was floating around in this blinding whiteness, moving the drapes, adjusting them, adjusting them. Everything so shimmering and lovely. The instruments in trays beside me, which I assumed were for the haircut, were pearly and beautiful. When the angel hovered close, I managed to say "Hi."

The angel, a French angel, was surprised. She smiled. In Frenchy English she said it was good I was with them, and good that my wife would soon come for a visit. But I must now rest, the angel said. Not to talk.

I am weightless. I don't try to move because my body is of no interest to me. I am only my thoughts and what I see. There are tubes coming and going from me, and there is a robotic row of blinking, beeping equipment beside me.

Time passes. The reef. My family. My leg must be gone by now. Of course. This is a nurse in Tahiti. The French words swirling around me are accounted for.

My family—I took inventory: When did I see each of them last? Did we all make it? What is real here, and what is dream? Were they all on the helicopter? How many kids do I have? Was anyone missing? Can I move my arms? *Oui.* Can I move my right leg? *Oui, un peu.* My left leg? Gone. *Kidnappé par des pirates. Mangé la baleine.* Gone, as I expected. So that is it. But I am alive, which is such a huge surprise. The shimmering of the curtain was like heaven.

And no pain.

Well, there is some—a dull report from a body that does not interest me.

So, where is my family? How are they? How is Ben's head? Jean was in *serious* shock; where is she? Ah! She is at my side, reaching carefully through the nest of tubes, trying to hug me when I see her and say, "God moves in a mysterious way, his wonders to perform...." Why did I just say that? Jean looked at me and smiled. We were both surprised by the words. Only later would I find out the rest of the verse that was written by an eighteenth-century poet, William Cowper. "He plants his footsteps in the sea, and rides upon the storm." She is also a patient in the hospital, she says. She feels the muscle of my arm and says I feel warm again. The kids are all right, she reports; they are down in the harbor on the *Fruity Fruits.* Ben has a bandaged head but is okay—he is hardheaded like me. Carolyne and Steffan are taking care of everyone. They have all been praying for me, Jean says. Surgery was a little touch and go, as so many of my organs were in failure. My brother Mark is on his way from the States, either to help me get out of here or to take my body home. How long ago was it when he busted me out of the hospital after I fell from that nuke-cooling tower? A lifetime. I'm not going to walk away from this one. Hop, maybe.

I'm waiting to watch myself have some big reaction to the fact that my leg is gone, but I really don't much care. It is just so damn spectacular to be back alive.

Dear Carolyne, half-French, had been in Jean's hospital room to translate and console her. Jean thought I was gone. She had prayed her goodbyes to me. The doctors, coming to her after surgery to make their report, seemed so sullen at first. She had tried to mentally prepare, but there is never any way to really do that. You just take it; you roll into it. But they suddenly smiled their little tight-lipped French doctor smiles and reported that I was, barring infection, *madame,* going to live—but they had of course taken my leg—*sa jambe, madame.* They took it from just below the knee. Little Jack, thinking ahead to future science fairs, had already asked for it but was turned down. She held me and we tried so hard not to laugh.

I would need dialysis and some other things for a few weeks. Yes, of course—unless brother Mark could spring me, is what I was thinking.

———

Poor thing, Jean was wearing an orange T-shirt with a neon-bright picture of a very scantily clad, big-busted woman—surrounded by a huge marijuana leaf. The caption read "It's a jungle out there." Jean is a little particular with her clothing. I dared not laugh at her; she probably hadn't looked down at herself to see what she had been given to wear on the little island. Castaway clothing for a castaway. This was her new, more economical look. And why not? Our big investment was drifting in a million flakes to the bottom of the sea, mixing there with the gold coins and children's bones of other families.

And in the short term? Passports, credit cards, cash, clothing, everything was gone. Carolyne was going boat to boat in the Tahiti yacht harbor collecting clothes for the kids and for Jean. Everything I see, hear, feel, and smell is new to me. It's all a wonder. You can say I should have known better, but I couldn't remember that.

Aye, aye, I know that he was never very jolly; and I know that on the passage home, he was a little out of his mind for a spell; but it was the sharp shooting pains in his bleeding stump that brought that about, as any one might see. I know, too, that ever since he lost his leg last voyage by that accursed whale, he's been a kind of moody—desperate moody, and savage sometimes; but that will all pass off.

—Herman Melville, MOBY DICK

[2]

COALS FROM NEWCASTLE

How on earth did we hit it, the reef? Hospitals are organized to wake you throughout the night and wake you again before dawn. If you need rest you must never go to a hospital. But my mind had enough of its own to keep me awake. I was lying there under my IVs and trying to figure out how it could have happened.

We were not the first to hit it, but, unlike the other known wreck, the *Julia Ann* in 1855, we had modern GPS and all that. And we had been watching so carefully. I just didn't get it.

The *Julia Ann* hit the reef almost exactly where we did. I would later study old accounts of the disaster to help make sense of our own experience. Maybe this research was a part of my rehabilitation, for that process takes a long time and you go through quite a bit. This ship, the *Julia Ann*, was our sister ship in the book of fate, and I became attached to her captain and crew and her passengers, who were remarkable people. We had shared a reef, shared a long night, and shared a sunrise.

So, yes, the *Julia Ann* hit the same reef. For what it's worth, they hit it, by Sydney time, on Jean's and my anniversary, October 4. But that was a very minor connection compared to what else I would soon learn.

They were being careful, too. Captain Pond had a lookout high in the foremast. This was a barque, which is a tall sailing ship with three or four jib sails out front on the bowsprit and three tall masts on deck. The first two masts are square-rigged, with three or four spars and square sails on each. The third mast, near the stern, called the mizzenmast, is gaff-rigged, meaning it has an irregular square sail—almost triangular—hung from a slantways boom mounted on the mast, quite like a Chinese junk's sail. That sail is sometimes called a spanker—it gives the ship an extra boost.

The *Julia Ann* was a big boat that could move very fast with a heavy cargo. It was bringing Australian coal from Newcastle, New South Wales, to Pacific ports and to California. Also aboard were a huddle of people heading back to the gold camps of California from the gold camps of Australia, and Australian-born Mormon missionaries heading to Utah for a big religious event. They were in the last generation to travel the seas by sail; steamers were on the way.

The *Julia Ann,* an American ship registered in San Francisco, was doing eleven and a half knots at about 8:00 p.m. when, just as the watch was changing and both helmsmen were below, the lookout shouted "hard down the helm"—but too late. Nobody had seen the reef, just as we hadn't. There were dozens of people on deck and a man in the mast and still they hadn't see it. They hit the same spot: the southern point of the heart-shaped ridge of coral that forms the heart-shaped lagoon. The coral thickens on the north to form a narrow island of palm trees, but in the south it is a simple long and deadly coral reef.

The captain thought he was sixteen miles clear of it, as did I.

It is so invisible, I think, because the waves, as they approach the steep underwater shoulder of the reef, hump up into a black wave that hides the reef entirely from behind. You just can't see the breaking surf or the reef until you are upon it. In daylight, you can often see the color difference of the lagoon ahead, but not at night. This particular reef, Scilly Island, is seven miles across its lagoon, so the waves breaking toward you on the farther reef are too distant to see.

So you rise over that black wave and there it is: the surprise test on every subject you know and everything you are. There is no time to rehearse; whoever you are in those next moments is exactly who you are. It is who your family is, too.

Captain Pond was actually quite brilliant in that moment. He didn't cut the sails, because he wanted the wind to drive the tall-masted ship as high as possible onto the reef; he knew that if she slid down now she would slide into the mile-deep water with most hands aboard. It was a smart decision for a big boat whose hull had likely already been breached, and whose history had already been written.

For myself, I took a moment to start the engines on the slight chance they could back us off the reef and we could escape this. Then the big waves lifted us up, lifted the propellers out of the water, and jammed us nose-first into the reef. But it had been worth trying.

There was so much history along the way. We had made a point of teaching the kids and ourselves everything as we sailed along. I am a chatterbox in that regard. We had been on the trail of Columbus and slavery, democracy and invasion, Spanish conquistadors, Darwin, Teddy Roosevelt and the Panama Canal, and pirates, of course. We were, toward the end, in *Mutiny on the Bounty* territory. The HMS *Bounty* had waited out the cyclone season in Tahiti, as had *Emerald Jane*. The *Bounty*'s men had, on that fabled isle, seen all the paradise they ever needed, and they didn't want to go back on the ship. They didn't want to have Bligh whipping and cursing them all the way back to England by way of the Horn of Africa and the Caribbean. So they did what they did. Leaving paradise is very hard and very dangerous. As they plotted the mutiny, they passed close to the reef where our journey ended—Bligh was a fabulous navigator— better, it turns out, than me and a GPS system.

Before I leave Bligh, let me comment that he was not really so bad. As a captain myself, with a sometimes lazy and insolent crew who once tossed me overboard, I could relate. Bligh's mission was to obtain a cargo of baby breadfruit trees, which grew on Tahiti, and fetch the live plants to where they could be grown to cheaply feed plantation slaves in the Caribbean. It was all arranged by a friend of Bligh's, the King's science adviser, Joseph Banks, who had sailed the South Pacific with the great Captain Cook—also through these same waters, uncharted at the time.

Banks, a most excitable naturalist who brings to mind my son Jack, was sailing with Cook to Tahiti because that was going to be the best place to observe the planet Venus on a critical night when its measure would help determine the diameter of the solar system. A grand voyage, with Cook and Banks so seduced by Tahiti that their logs overflowed. After meeting up with Venus, they explored the Society Islands, presumably including Scilly, on their way west to New Zealand. Later, Cook returned and came through the area on his way to find, if he could, a "northwest passage" above North America. His young navigator and mapmaker was Mr. Bligh, then twenty-three. Captain Cook, unfortunately, was killed by the Hawaiians on that voyage.

In his own ship later, Bligh first tried to get to Tahiti by going around South America. But after battling storms at the Cape for thirty days, he retreated and went around Africa instead. A lesser captain might have risked his crew and pushed ahead through the storm. Bligh let his forty-five-man crew sleep in his own huge stateroom to get out of the cold storm, and he didn't lose a man or make his ship suffer a dent or rip. It was a small ship, the *Bounty*, though it was indeed tall and beautiful. It was sturdy, built for the coal trade. She was twice as long as our *Emerald Jane*, but only just as wide—and some 215 tons. The *Julia Ann*, also a coal trader, which we followed into the reef, was some 375 tons.

In Bligh's further defense, it should be noted that he let his men rest for thirty days following those storms. For their entertainment, he had hired for the journey a blind Irish fiddler by the name of Michael Byrne so that the men might dance their nightly jigs and keep fit. Who, then, was ever a better captain than Bill Bligh? He also carried the right food, sauerkraut and lots of it, to keep the men healthy and scurvy-free. And when a few men went AWOL in Tahiti, he gave them a dozen or two lashes instead of the usual punishment, which was the lashes plus hanging until dead from the yardarm. So he was almost excessively indulgent. He did have a bit of a temper, and that was his undoing, but captains can empathize.

In our last evening on the sea, we sailed among the ghosts of mariners past, roaming between Australia and Hawaii, where the HMS *Bounty* had traveled westward from Tahiti on her way to trouble, where gold-seekers and missionaries and so many others had sailed eastward from the Horn of Africa and from Sydney to the promise of the American West. I could feel that history upon the sea.

But here is where history caught up with us. Here is where we would have to live out our own mortal adventure on this planet and not just observe. Here we would share a story with the frightened souls of the *Julia Ann*. If you want to know what it was like for the people of the *Julia Ann* that night, and in the days following, you can simply crash your boat where they crashed theirs and suffer as they suffered, and that's the best way to learn.

You need not go that far, but my point is that getting an education is about getting out into the world and seeing and feeling the planet for yourself. Television doesn't cut it. If real life catches you by the heel sometimes, it is worth it. Life is short anyway, so it may as well be beautiful.

And *Moby Dick*! A novel, of course, not history, but I *so understood that story now*. What a course it was in literature that long night! I understood now how you can pay a great price to be so compelled to meet Life head on, how you can tangle in your own ropes and go down with the monster, or nearly so, and how it can take your leg or as much as seems right for this sacrifice to Life. It will eventually get all of you, so why wait around half-dead somewhere when you can get into it right now for the small price of a limb or what have you? And the *Pequod,* Captain Ahab's ship, dreamed up by Melville's genius pen, sailed to its imaginary end just up on the equator northwest of our doom.

So much to think about as the days ticked away; the kids, my brother, and friends came to visit, the doctors conferred in French, Jean hugged me for hours as the morning and afternoon sun of Papeete, Tahiti, streamed through the old windows.

I can surely stand on that reef in my mind. I can stand with my peg leg under the stars on the ledge Ben found for his family. I can look at the wreck of the *Emerald Jane,* surely, but I can also see the barque *Julia Ann* speeding toward the reef. I can hear the man atop the mast calling out his warning. I can hear the yelling and screaming on deck and the great roar of all that timber and sea as she comes at full speed upon the reef. I can see it better than any man alive, except my children and my wife, who are similarly well educated in this regard.

You have seen old, square-rigged ships like the *Julia Ann* in any ship-in-a-bottle: The deck up near the bow is raised a few steps. That is the foredeck, and, another few steps up, is a smaller deck at the very tip of the bow called the forecastle, pronounced *fokes'l.* From there extends the bowsprit, which is the great forward-slanting mast at the tip of the ship which holds four or five long-triangle jib sails. Amidships is the main deck, filled with masts and lines. The back quarter of the ship's deck is raised about eight feet and is called the quarterdeck. At the front of the quarterdeck is a steering house, surrounded with windows. The main wheel and the charts are inside. Another wheel is outside and in front of the house, enclosed by an iron railing. Farther back on the quarterdeck, a few steps up at the very stern, is the poop deck. The name comes not from the biological utility of its location, but from the Spanish and Middle English word for "stern"—although there may be a roundabout connection. Underneath the quarter- and poop decks is a very large, partitionable space called the great cabin, where you would find first-class passengers in times of peace and cannons in times of war.

Fifty-six passengers heading the impossibly long way from Sydney Harbor to San Francisco Bay gathered at 2:00 p.m. on the lower deck amidships and sang hymns as the lines were cast and the ship was pulled out into the harbor by rowboat tugs. It was Friday, September 7, 1855. The weather was gray and drippy.

The assembled passengers on deck, and some of the seventeen crewmen now scrambling high above them in the rigging, sang "The Gallant Ship Is Under Way," a hymn based on an old poem by Robert Southey. It was commonly sung in joyful tones, but sounded more like a dirge this day. Perhaps that was because of the steely weather, or perhaps a sense of foreboding still hung over the ship from its eighty-three-day passage on the same route the previous year, which had met high seas, contrary winds, great seasickness, a measles outbreak, and the death of a pregnant mother. And, of course, some passengers were now leaving family behind on the dock whom they would not see again for many years or forever. Going to another continent in 1855 was like going to another planet.

Among the passengers were several children and infants. I can see them on the deck in my mind's eye. I can see my Jack there, running up and down the steps of the poop deck until Captain Pond shouts for someone to please, in the name of God, cage that monkey. I can see Camille waving to everyone on the dock, blowing kisses. I can see Amelia looking around with a critical eye at all the little kids on board, knowing she will probably be pressed into service to care of them before long. She would notice ten-year-old Marion Anderson as someone almost old enough to play with. I can see Jean near the rail, her arms folded, looking up and around at the whole setup. She is nicely dressed.

Many of the *Julia Ann's* passengers were Mormons, two being church missionary officials and twenty-six others being recent Mormon converts from Australia. The Mormons were heading to Utah by way of California. Delivering Mormons to Utah may seem like taking "coals to New-castle," but that would only be right for this voyage, as the ship's other cargo was in fact coal, 350 tons of it, from Newcastle, New South Wales. The ship would therefore not lack for ballast, physical and spiritual, to keep her upright in the hard winds ahead.

Casting off this September morning—which is early spring Down Under—was complex work, fraught with a rash of little errors by the crew. Captain Pond's angry commands could not have helped the mood of the passengers. He had to have been aware, as I was, of the ancient sailing superstition that it is bad luck to leave on a voyage on Friday. Both the *Julia Ann* and the *Emerald Jane* pulled out of port on a Friday. Each for our own reasons ignoring the superstition.

"The day seemed very unpropitious and gloomy and before our anchor was weighed it commenced blowing and raining, and in getting out of the harbor we met with very many annoying accidents," wrote Captain Pond. In fact, it would be remarkable if setting sail could ever be accomplished without some mishaps. Imagine the captain's call, "Men aloft," followed by a swarm of hands heading for the rail, then all of them swinging out over the water, pulling themselves up the tall triangles of rope-ladder-like rigging with amazing speed and strength. They rise to the various tops, which are like crow's nests, but are at various levels up each mast where the great rope ladders terminate. From these stations, they make their ways like monkeys out along the horizontal spars. Some young sailors scoot out carefully, using the scallop-looped foothold ropes dangling from the spars, while some skinny old sailors literally run atop the spars like circus acrobats then drop down to the foot loops when they reach their positions. A precise and complex set of shouts from the captain or the first mate will have these men working in unison, each holding on to a spar with one hand and hauling sail with the other. How it is all done without serious accident—for it usually is—must count as a marvel of our species.

Ships must usually be pulled out toward the entrance of the harbor before they stretch out their canvas to the wind. Our own little ship, of course, had diesel engines for that purpose.

> *The gallant ship is under way*
> *To bear me off to sea.*
> *And yonder float the streamers gay*
> *That say she waits for me.*
> *The seamen dip their ready oar,*
> *As ebbing waves oft tell;*
> *They bear me swiftly from the shore.*
> *My native land, farewell!*

Out there finally in the breeze, a little away from the smoke and exploitations of the city, the sudden thump of the breeze catching the canvas and the gentle lean of the boat freshens up one's youthful remnants; it is a holiday morning and all the big and little reversals suffered while getting under way are now but ancient history. Slowly at first the sea slaps at the hull, which becomes a rushing curl of water and then a wake. And soon you are off into the grand ocean, following your dreams.

Indeed, the California Gold Rush was only six years old, and Australia's gold strike was only three years old, so the flow of gold-seekers back and forth across the Pacific, with geologists and smelter men and equipment, was furious and profitable trade for the *Julia Ann*. Australia was still partly a penal colony, so those who had served their terms and now wanted to get to America to dig gold, or for any other dream, were not in short supply in the harbors where the tall ships would lay in for passengers. The steerage fare to California, twenty-four pounds sterling, was a fortune, but you could work as a laborer for a third- or half-year and save it up. Or if you knew sailing, you could work your way across, which was the case with Mormon Charles Logie, who got his family aboard in exchange for his own hard labor.

Like half the passengers on the *Julia Ann,* the Logies were not dreaming of California gold, but a more heavenly treasure:

> *I go but not to plough the main*
> *To ease a restless mind,*
> *Nor do I toil on battle's plain*
> *The victor's wreath to twine.*
> *'Tis not for treasures that are hid*
> *In mountain or in dell.*
> *'Tis not for joys like these I bid*
> *My native land, farewell!*
>
> *I go because my Master calls;*
> *He's made my duty plain*
> *No danger can the heart appall*
> *When Jesus stoops to reign!*
> *And now the vessel's side we've made,*
> *The sails their bosoms swell;*
> *Thy beauties in the distance fade*
> *My native land, farewell!*

The *Julia Ann* headed straight into big weather and seasickness. Mothers held their sick children, and the company bravely sang their hymns above- and belowdecks. After two weeks tossing—in every sense—they entered the calmer waters east of New Zealand to find the winds that would take them across the wide Pacific. We followed the trade winds across, coming the other way from Tahiti.

On the twenty-sixth night, Captain Pond set a course through the first sprinkling of the Society Islands.

All that day he had kept extra lookouts for reefs. There were decent charts for these waters, some made by William Bligh himself and widely used, but there were still times when something new would be seen, or some error in a chart would put a boat aground. Any defect in the ship's clock, or any unsteadiness in the hand holding the quadrant or sextant to the horizon could put the ship off its intended course by many miles.

By the same token, it now occurs to me that Bligh, so careful to have his mates chart the seas he sailed, had a demoralized crew—even a demoralized first mate, Fletcher Christian—on board through these waters. Did they care to take the readings just right? Did they care to help preserve their captain's high reputation for mapmaking? Or were they fast and careless with the sextant as they stood on Bligh's quarterdeck to measure the stars from the horizon? Could the impending mutiny on the *Bounty* have led to a map error that led the *Julia Ann* astray? And were the old maps *we* were using correct, or did they preserve this old error, if any there was? Our charts went down with the *Emerald Jane*. I expect our chart was derived from a more modern source, and our error came from elsewhere, but I do not know that for certain. We thought our *Emerald Jane* was located right about where Pond thought the *Julia Ann* was located, when, in fact, we were upon the reef. History, as I have said, can catch up with you. I do not know the answer. Bligh, in any case, would not have been the first to map the island, as the British seaman Samuel Wallis had sighted it twenty-two years earlier. Even so, if there had been an error in Wallis's map that was not corrected by the *Bounty* because of its distractions, we still have a good and curly question to put at the service of a storytelling father.

Pond, trusting no map, watched even with his own eyes much of the day, and, as it was reported, he was worried and moody. The area around Scilly Island is particularly tricky, as that reef and others are submerged at high tide and hard to see, even by day. But they are never so submerged they cannot rip the bottom from a ship and send it to doom in moments.

Pond had ordered full canvas to get through the area before dark, but there were still miles to go as night fell for the last time on the *Julia Ann*. He sent a man high aloft and then he rechecked their position and the map. Sail on in the dark they must, for a great ship cannot be left to bob in the ocean through the night, as there are no shallows for a steadying anchorage. Drifting, the ship may find a reef anyway. Simply slowing down will not help much, as there is no such thing as a minor collision with a reef in the night. So they sped on at a remarkable eleven and a half knots. That converts to a little more than thirteen miles per hour, but it is racing speed for such a boat, controlled, as it is, by dozens of men and hundreds of lines.

At 7:30 in the evening, the sea became broken, which means irregular: smooth here and choppy there. There are all kinds of seas, by the way, and a ship's log will record them throughout the day and night, along with wind and temperature and sky. These, in the days before radio and satellite, would be reported at landfalls or at the final destination, so that other mariners might see the latest. A sea may be smooth, long-rolling, chopping, cross-cutting, moderate, heavy, rough, or, as I cited, broken, meaning irregular. It was that.

At sundown, Captain Pond scanned the horizon and saw no land. Scilly was sixteen miles off to port, according to his quadrant measurements and the charts. It would be clear sailing through the night, he thought. He went below to get some rest after the stressful day of constant watch. He ordered a change of watch so the fresh eyes of a rested helmsman would be on duty through the first hours of the night. Mr. Coffin prepared to relieve Mr. Logie at the helm. Mr. Coffin was an experienced whaler who had commanded his own ships, and Pond trusted him second only to himself in dangerous waters. Mr. Coffin, at the helm now, fumbled in the pockets of his wool coat to find his spectacles, which his years now demanded. He had left them by his bunk. He went below to find them, leaving the wheel to a mate.

The children, most of them, were asleep below, tended by their mothers. Most of the other passengers were on deck taking the evening air. The situation below was always crowded and terribly stuffy, especially in the steerage section, where passage was cheapest and most crowded.

Separated into areas for single men, single women, and married families with their children, the steerage was a low-ceilinged hive of dark caverns filled with rough-timber bunk beds and areas for trunks and crates of belongings. Long tables were set out for communal meals, and kitchens were set up for families to cook their own shares of the weekly rations. Passengers in the aft cabin had it only slightly better. In decent weather, up on deck was the only pleasant place to be.

The night was dark; the stars were snuffed by the clouds, and the moon had not yet risen. I know the darkness they were seeing on deck: It has a thick and smothering seriousness to it, as if you were sailing at the edge of space and time itself. They would have lanterns lit on deck to make modest halos of gold and brown, but the void beyond the rail would have been, as it is, remarkably intense.

There is a sweetness to the moment just before hard fate falls upon men. I am standing in the door of our stateroom, so full of pride in my just-finished conversation with Amelia in the dark of the helm. I am sharing my report of it with my beautiful wife. She loves me enough to smile and set down her laptop, pausing the Tom Hanks movie she was watching. That moment floats in my mind. I see by lantern light the people on the *Julia Ann*'s deck. They are sitting on the steps to the roof of the steering house and on the steps of the poop deck; some are poised against the iron railing and some of the men—the nonmissionary half, anyway—are taking a cigar or pipe and sharing swigs from their flasks. They are talking and laughing a little about their big plans for California. They talk about their brothers and sisters already there, the situations awaiting them. They make thin promises to meet up and help each other in America. Some are in groups singing to pass the evening—led by the missionaries.

Hard down the helm. It is sad to end the scene, but, *Hard down the helm.* The words come screaming from the lookout on high at 8:30. Most passengers don't understand what this means. Then, God help them, they do.

[3]

THE *JULIA ANN*'S FATE

The collision came with the roar of thunder and a shock to the hull so violent that the passengers went sprawling across the decks, grabbing for holds and for each other. Captain Pond jumped from his bed, but a second thunderous turn sent him headlong across his stateroom floor.

A cavernous hole had already opened in the hull, and timber flew through the surf. The ocean picked up the boat and swung its stern and port quarter hard against the coral reef. The sea crashed in great waves over the top of the decks, creating a panic and a screaming that could hardly be heard above the roar of the surf and the booming impact of the breaking ship. Since it was impossible to stand up in the exploding surf, many of the passengers rushed below.

As they crowded down, Captain Pond fought his way up to the deck. With lanterns held overboard, he understood that the *Julia Ann,* which he half-owned, was lost. Some of the crew came to him for the order to cut the sails. He paused for a moment to try to think clearly. No. Leave the canvas up; it might help keep the broken ship from falling into the sea now. He shouted for the passengers to get into the great cabin in the aft section—which he took to be the strongest position. The great cabin, as I mentioned, is a large area under the quarterdeck commonly partitioned into rooms for the higher-paying passengers in peacetime. Because it may also become a cannon deck, it is built exceedingly strong.

In the glimmer of the remaining lanterns and mostly in the dark, there followed a mad scene of terror as mothers found their children and clutched them to their breasts as they fought their way through the surf-pounded deck for the great cabin. The passengers screamed to the crew, asking what they should do to save themselves and their children.

"Find something that might float, Miss, and cling to it," was the best the rushing men could offer, as no lifeboat could be launched upon a coral reef. The huge waves had already ripped them from their davits and taken them, except the quarter boat, which hung beside the quarterdeck and was normally used as a shuttle when at anchorage.

There was pandemonium below, as water was rushing into the steerage cabins now. Andrew and Elizabeth Anderson pulled seven of their eight children out of their beds as water flooded the compartment and crates and trunks floated violently in the wrenching movements of the ship. Andrew's leg was badly injured in this. He nevertheless fought through the water, carrying and leading his family across the wild deck to the great cabin. Their ten-year-old daughter, Marion, had been up on deck at the time of the crash and was up there yet. Andrew, after pushing his family into a corner of the great cabin, returned to the deck but could not find her in the dark chaos.

Miss Esther Spangenberg, a bright and well-traveled woman— she was not a missionary woman but made many friends among them—came on deck to see what had happened. I cannot help but think of and see my Amelia when I consider Esther Spangenberg. On the quarterdeck, above the great cabin, she squeezed her body between the iron railing and a bitt post, which is like a massive hitching post where lines aloft tie down to the deck, so that she could look overboard without being bucked off into the coral and the sea. From the lantern light streaming out through the portholes of the great cabin below, she could see the damage to the ship, the shattered slab of the rudder, the red teeth of the coral, and the great waves crashing into the hull and breaking it.

The boom of the spanker sail behind her broke from its mooring and swung wildly from the mizzenmast. It found her head just as she looked up from her inspection. It should have killed her but it did not—a glancing blow. She recovered her mind and her grip just in time to save herself from a huge wave that swept the deck and put her underwater, clinging to one of the two bitt posts.

In that moment, another young woman, Mary Humphries, and the ten-year-old daughter of the Andersons, little Marion, high on the poop deck, lost their hold under the great wave. They tumbled in the waterfall down to the coral, where they were tossed about like rag dolls and then sucked out to sea. Their screams, if there were such, were covered by the booming surf and the wail of heartbroken witnesses. They drowned and their bodies fell down the long, underwater cliff of the reef, down, down the dark mile to the bottom.

When the giant wave washed clear, Esther gave up her hold on the bitt post and made her way below to find a spot where she might peacefully meet her end while thinking of the friends she loved. That was prayer enough for her.

Mr. Pond was on the quarterdeck, as was right for a captain, holding the rail against the bucking of the ship and the towering floods. "The vessel was laboring and thumping in a most fearful manner, and it was almost impossible to cling to the iron railing upon the quarterdeck," he recorded.

Passenger John McCarthy, who would survive, wrote: "I saw mothers nursing their babes in the midst of falling masts and broken spars, while the breakers were rolling twenty feet high over the wreck."

Their hard night was just beginning.

[4]

THE LIFELINE

The *Julia Ann* was locked, stern-first, a little to port, into the red teeth of the coral, much as the *Emerald Jane* in her final hours. She was listing hard to starboard, bowing to the incoming surf, and coming apart with each great breaker. Thick in the surf now were great timbers, turned to new service as battering rams against their former compatriots in the hull.

A great wave was finally too much for the remaining rowboat, the quarter boat, which was ripped from its davits on the quarterdeck and sent into the raging water and coral. Our "quarter boat"—our dinghy—lost in exactly the same way. Remarkably, Second Mate Owens and a handful of crewmen leapt after it. They were swept off into the sharp coral, but they scrambled to save themselves and the small boat. Owens was seriously wounded by the coral and he lay for a time on a high shelf of coral, looking dead to his mates, but he recovered himself enough to be of use later, as did the other men overboard.

It is odd that they could see anything. I know what this is, from our own experience. Yes, there were still some lanterns in the portholes of the

Julia Ann, for the passengers were now assembled in the great cabin and the light would have been shining from those ports. But it is also true that the sea has its own light. There is always enough plankton in the water—the microscopic creatures that feed whales and the coral—to provide some bioluminescence when great waves crash. It is often not enough to notice on even a moonlit night, but here, with no stars even, it gave a glow to the whole scene. The plankton, so many generations later, did the same service for us, for which I thank them and their Creator.

Seeing that the men had survived in the water, Captain Pond called some hands around him and, shouting over the violent noise of the occasion, asked for a volunteer to go overboard with a strong line, toward the goal of attaching it to a high shelf of coral. In learning this history, I saw the wisdom of my own son. Yes, Captain Pond had some age in his eyes. But I can only see Ben.

Responding to Pond's suggestion, a crewman stripped off his shirt and placed a coil of rope about his neck. He grabbed the same dangling spanker boom that had cracked Miss Spangenberg on the head and he swung out over the churning coral. Lowering himself, he then made his way with great difficulty through the cutting edges and great waves until he found a high ledge and a sturdy coral post where he could tie the rope.

While the sea broke constantly over the ledge found by the mate of the *Julia Ann,* the ledge found by a mate of the *Emerald Jane* was higher and drier.

I would guess that the crew still aboard cut rope into loops that might be used as little bosun's chairs on the rope, so that by sitting in the loop and gripping the rope above, hand-over-hand, one might scoot from the poop deck, where I believe the rope was anchored aboard, to the high coral. The accounts are not specific here, but something like that was managed, and the passengers began to move, one by one, from the disintegrating ship. It was said to be "exceedingly arduous, and attended with much peril."

The first passenger to make the trip was given, by Pond's hand, the ship's sextant, a map, and the epitome, which is the little book that translates the sextant's star sightings to map positions. If any were to survive this night, and then attempt an escape by raft or by found rowboat, they would need these articles to survive. He charged this man with the duty of doing nothing more once upon the reef than to guard these items from harm. Here was a man, this Captain Pond, ready indeed for his moment of clear thinking and sudden, right action.

To avoid a rush for the rope, he had his mates contain the passengers in the great cabin until each family's name was called aloud from the passenger manifest. They were then escorted up to the quarterdeck, and then farther up to the poop deck and to the rope. For most of this, the boat was nearly stern-first into the reef, tilted to starboard.

By summoning names from the list, Pond and his men were able to move the women and children first, along with the husbands and fathers to help on the rope. There was a constant, hard-boiling panic in the room as the names were slowly called, for the sea began to take the starboard side of the room, and the people had then to struggle to not slide down the flooded floor into the maw of the surf. Waiting rooms are uncomfortable in any case, but this was one of a kind.

> *And when my pilgrim feet shall tread*
> *On land where darkness dwells,*
> *Where light and truth have long since fled*
> *My native land, farewell!*

Esther Spangenberg, who had not found a peaceful place to die while thinking of her friends, was in the great cabin now and she recorded:

When I reached the cabin, the scene that presented itself to my view can never be erased from my memory: Mothers screaming and children clinging to them in terror and dread; the furniture torn from its lashings and all upturned; the ship was lying on her beam ends; the starboard side of her was opening, and the waves were washing in and out of the cabin.

When families were brought through the flash floods of the deck to the rope, some were panic-stricken to see the difficulty ahead—a storm-whipped line leading down into the volcano of red coral and froth, and disappearing into the dark. A family of four was at the rope looking when the boat twisted on the reef and seemed to be coming fully apart. The father took to the rope alone, leaving his family behind. When he got to the reef, the crew mates there, who had seen it happen in the distant lantern glow on deck, threw him back into the raging surf to drown. But he was instead washed up in the next wave to another ridge of coral, where he was allowed to cower and cry—the mates had pressing duties and could not work a court of justice, too.

Aboard, Captain Pond urged the woman to save herself and leave the children with him. That the ship was now disintegrating was clear. She shook her head in resignation and in shame for her husband, and she led her children back to the great cabin to wait for death.

Another father at the rope had tied his baby to his back and he then held his seventeen-year-old wife in his arms as he traveled the rope to the reef, all to the great admiration and encouraging cheers of the waiting crew members manning the far bottom of the rope.

The great ship was sliding off the reef, stretching the hauling rope ever tighter until, at a fortunate moment when no one was upon it, it broke. It was quickly replaced with a new line and more passengers were urged to take it down.

A young girl appeared on deck at the line without her mother, who was nowhere to be found. A trusted crew member, Second Mate Owens, was leaving the boat at that moment with a small sack in his embrace. In this sack, as the Captain had requested, was the liquid portion of Pond's life savings from the ship's safe: four hundred gold coins. Pond stopped the man from doing him this service and had him instead take the girl across. The tight bag plopped across the listing deck and slipped into the sea without deflecting Pond's attention, now directed toward the next candidate for the repaired rope.

The rope would break twice more as the boat slipped farther into the sea. Each time it was replaced, but each time the gulf between the deck and the high coral widened. Some passengers refused to take their turn, fearing they would be swept from the line or that the water washing over the reef would drown them, even if they crossed the chasm.

Captain Pond and his officers begged the remaining passengers to be brave and save themselves, warning them that the ship would slip into the sea at any moment. It was this identical premonition that forced my hand, asking Ben to free me from the mast with his knife. I wasn't yet ready to buy into going down with my ship.

[5]

THE THIRD BREAK

Esther Spangenberg, who had emotionally prepared herself to die, decided to survive if she possibly could. By that time, the sea had broken the ship severely, tearing away the stairs up to the quarterdeck where the rope was again repaired and ready. A fit woman, she exited the great cabin and then had to obtain to the higher quarterdeck by grabbing hold of one of the many swinging rigging lines and swinging up as if on a vine. She recorded:

> The Captain and officers had great difficulty in persuading the greater number of the ladies. As for myself, I considered to remain on the ship was sure death, and I might save my life by trying to reach the reef by means of the rope. I therefore bade my fellow passengers farewell, and reached the deck by swaying myself there with a rope, the steps being gone. I was assisted over the side of the ship by some of the crew, and directed how to haul on by the rope. After considerable difficulty, I reached the reef, my clothes torn in shreds, and my person bruised and mangled. But I was fortunate in escaping, even in that plight.

Even now, in thinking of their night, I can only imagine it properly by remembering the great noise of our own boat breaking up, of the thunder and rush of the waves on deck, and of our great worry for each other. Words fail me, but memory serves me well to emotionally understand what they were experiencing.

When the rope was replaced the third time, and the ship was teetering on the edge of the underwater precipice, Pond begged those still cowering in the great cabin to come up and be saved. The ship was now twice as far from the high coral as when the rope operation was begun, and the crew, except for Pond and First Mate Coffin, were off the ship now, helping those on the coral.

Eliza Harris and Martha Humphries now decided they would try the rope. Both of them were traveling without their husbands, who were scheduled to sail on a subsequent voyage. Eliza had with her a two-year-old daughter, Maria, and a six-month-old son, Lister. She strapped her tiny son to her chest and told her daughter to hold tight to her neck. Before she could swing over the rail to the rope, a huge wave hit the boat. The little girl was saved, but Eliza and baby Lister were swept away forever.

This same great wave broke the boat in two, sending up shrieks of horror from those remaining in the great cabin, for the starboard side of that cabin was lost now, too, taking Martha Humphries to her death. As she was pulled away in the great withdrawal of the wave and debris, she called to those remaining to take care of her children, please, that her own "earthly career is run."

I go devoted to His cause,
And to His will resigned;
His presence will supply the loss
Of all I leave behind.
His promise cheers the sinking heart,

And lights the darkest cell,
To exiled pilgrims grace imparts
My native land, farewell!

The main break came at the cargo hatch; the fore section of the ship now only lightly connected to the aft. Water rushed full into the great cabin now, and the occupants were helped up to the quarterdeck above, where they stared at the hellish swirl below the rope.

The rope was again stretched to about its breaking point. There would be no replacing it from this extended distance.

Pond was certain now that the remaining section was likely to turn upside down at any moment—certainly with the next great wave. Nineteen passengers huddled now on the deck, and they would not move. Some were too horrified to speak, while others were praying and seemed prepared to die. Some held their crying children close.

Pond must have explained that he also had an obligation to the people on the reef, and that he must tend to them if these people would not allow themselves to be saved. He must, knowing him as we do, have knelt and implored them again, but they would not go. It should be noted that the gulf between the deck and the high coral was now very great and the sea was very dark and fierce. So it may have seemed to some that the captain was asking them to kill themselves, when they might yet be safe in this high place.

Pond and Coffin used the rope then to move to the reef themselves. Soon after, the line broke for the last time.

On the reef, Pond noticed young Agnes Anderson sitting on the broken main mast that had fallen across the coral. All her living family was yet aboard. Through the roaring surf, Pond heard the child's mother, now on the hopelessly stranded poop deck—call through the storm, "Agnes, Agnes, come to me!" It was a piercing wail as if from another world. The mother may have been calling to the dark sea, thinking her daughter lost, or she may have wanted them all to go to paradise together that night. In any case, obedient young Agnes leapt up from the mast, calling, "I am coming, Mother," and slid into the churning water to return to the ship. By her hem, she was caught by a quick sailor and held tightly.

[6]

THE MONSTER

It was around 1:00 a.m. when the wave they would call the monster came. There was a great crying out from the people on board and those on the reef who watched. The wave finished the breaking of the ship, creating a great slurry of beams and spars in a rolling flood of final destruction as main pieces of the *Julia Ann* were sucked into the deep. Great prayers and calls for mercy were said separately but full aloud by all, and, in this moment, the full breaking of the hull spilled the cargo of coal into the sea, which buoyed the remaining quarterdeck and poop deck up like a mighty raft, revealed suddenly by the moon slipping free from the black clouds. It was carried high and flat upon the great wave and set down on the coral close by to where the escaped passengers and crew were gathered in the chest-high shallows. In this way, the saints and sinners clinging to the rails of the decks and to each other and to their children were all saved, and a great cheering then raised up over the thundering surf.

Yet on His mighty arm I trust
That makes the feeble strong.
My sun, my shield forever nigh,
He will my fears dispel!

The ship's wheel was still mounted on the quarterdeck, which was now a treehouse in the branches of coral. Though submerged to a depth of three feet, the deck was sturdy enough to attract all the souls who would fit upon it—who were not elsewhere perched on fallen masts or planks. The ship's bell was still mounted on the deck, and, with each roll of the surf, it tolled. It tolled through the moonlit night for the five lost: for the two little children and the three ladies.

Except for these, the rest, the fifty-one passengers and seventeen crew members, were saved.

Or were they? They were shipwrecked now on a tiny, off-course reef in the vast South Pacific. They were now standing in deep water, their limbs and arms bleeding, with countless sharks now visible in the moonlight. There was wailing and loud praying, for the waves washed up to their necks and all knew that a monster wave might wash them away: "Cold, naked and dispirited, women lamenting, children crying, and none of us certain but the next moment would be our last," recorded Esther Spangenberg.

Captain Pond, half-floating in the water, dozed off from exhaustion. He woke near dawn and saw this, as he later recorded:

The moon was up and shed her faint light over the dismal scene; the sullen roar of the breakers sent an additional chill through my already benumbed frame. The bell at the wheel, with every surge of the sea, still tolled a knell to the departed, and naught else but the wailings of a bereaved mother broke the stillness of the night, or indicated life among that throng of human automata; during the long hours of that weary night the iron had entered their souls, and the awful solemnity of their situation was brooded over in silence.

[7]

A SHARED DAWN

As the long night became pale dawn and high tide receded before them, the *Julia Ann's* crew and passengers alike began to comb the coral for supplies that might prove useful or edible in the coming hours, days, or—who could know how long? Little piles were growing on the higher ledges of coral.

This sort of scavenger hunt, which Ben would replay a century and a half later, gives the mind and body something positive to do. It is our human adaptability kicking into gear. A new life, if only a short one, can be assembled from these broken parts, bits of food, and memories. Ben was thinking we might be on this reef for a long time. He first needed some boards and cushions for his family to sit on, as the reef was so sharp. Then some food, water bottles. He found his contact lens supply. He found a plastic box of secondary flares. Jean was so safety-conscious that we even had emergency flares in case the main emergency flares got lost or used up or too wet. When the jet came over, Ben took one of these backup flares, as the regular flare gun was on the ledge, a ways away from where he was scavenging.

There was only one shot left in that anyway, after the potshots at the moon.

With these other flares, which were about the size of a dinner candle, you pulled a pin out of the base and pushed a button. Ben thought it would light up in his hand like a highway flare. So, when the jet was spotted and he scrambled to figure it out, he was a little surprised when it kicked in his hand like a shotgun, sending its red fire into the sky and thankfully not into his eye. But the thing worked. They saw it in the dawn light.

For the survivors of the *Julia Ann*, the dawn light revealed a distant line of palm trees on the horizon—the sun would rise right through the trees, as it had for us. In that 150 years the view had not changed. For them as for us, it meant hope after a desperate night.

The quarter boat, which had been rescued by Pond's crew, was in one piece but had a bad hole made by its tumble to the coral. The ship's carpenter, who had collected his most vital tools and a pocketful of nails before he climbed down the rope those hard hours ago, found bits of canvas and copper to quickly patch the boat. A party, led by Pond, then set out to explore the distant island, nearly eight miles off through the lagoon—and they quickly noted its beauty. Pond's departure raised the fears of the passengers, who can be forgiven their newfound fear of abandonment. The captain assured them he would return soon with a full report. Fresh water and dry land must be found soon, he reminded them, and he was off on that quest.

It is most interesting to me that the quarter boat plied the exact waters that the men of the Taputu family would in a similar boat to come help us. Honestly, it was not what Jean wanted to see. She had hoped the next sighting after the French Navy jet would be a helicopter to whisk me to a trauma center. She wanted out of this paradise, and that is never easy.

In fact, there was a helicopter warming up, a mere 350 miles away. A Super Puma search-and-rescue helicopter waited on the tarmac in Tahiti.

In the cockpit, Captain Sebastien Roger and his copilot, Captain Yves Peltrault, waited patiently for the word. The sun had risen. They had been alerted late the night before and had arrived early to plan the operation and wait for the report from the French Navy jet.

There had been conflicting information from the New Zealand and Australian Rescue Coordination Centers to the effect that our beacon may have been a false alarm, so a visual confirmation had been ordered. Finally, confirmation from the jet: wreckage spotted on the reef, survivors in the water.

"Finalement," Captain Roger said into the intercom. *"Prêt à partir."*

Copilot Peltrault spun up the two, giant, four-bladed props atop the big copter and they were off.

In the cabin, the team's doctor, Médecin Chef Bruno Volpeliere, checked his watch. With a Bora-Bora fuel stop after ninety minutes of flying, they would probably not reach the wreck until late morning. Not a problem; there had been no reports of injuries. It was a long reach for a rescue helicopter.

As they left, the Taputu family's little boat approached us closer and closer across the vast turquoise lagoon.

Their boat looked oddly lopsided to Jean. They had piggybacked a rowboat sideways across the middle of their motorboat to help bring us all back across in one trip. Also, they would use the smaller boat to get through the maze of coral between the lagoon and our position.

The six boys and men anchored out on a sand flat, and four of them then paddled the dinghy toward our coral ledge.

They smiled broadly and called out: "Bonjour, M'dame. Bonjour, les enfants."

Jean was looking for a doctor and listening for a helicopter.

The men carefully but quickly climbed over the coral and dipped into the small pool where I was floating in the raft. They poked their heads inside. I was a little delusional anyway, so they were interesting to see. The men became serious as they now understood it was not an easy, joyful rescue.

Jean was wearing only her bra and a pair of shorts. Her shirt had been donated to help keep me warm, along with much of the kid's clothing.

"T'a besoin d'une chemise?" the older man asked, unbuttoning his shirt to give her. He was a big, strong-looking man with a slightly graying ponytail, a bushy salt-and-pepper mustache, and a gold tiki pendant on a leather strand around his neck. Wearing blues and greens against his brown skin, he looked entirely of the Polynesian sea. If *GQ* would do a South Pacific issue, he could be the cover. It now occurred to Jean that the man was the father of these other men; this was a family.

"Pauvre monsieur" (poor fella), the old man muttered, staring down at my leg. He and his boys reached into the raft to raise me out.

"No, monsieur!" Jean shouted. She worried that a sudden move like that would finish me off, and she was still expecting paramedics to drop out of the sky. After all, we're Americans. Sometimes Jean expects a lot. Our employees in the home-building business just loved that about her. Of course a fireplace can be moved.

She mimed instructions for them to move me and the raft together, which they did. They balanced the life raft on their dinghy and gave Camille a ride in the tiny room remaining in the bow. Everyone else then began the difficult half-mile journey through the coral to the lagoon, where the motor launch awaited at anchor.

On the way, the father introduced his family to Jean and the kids. He tapped his big chest and pointed to his sons. "Taputu," he said. "La Famille Taputu…"

"Silverwood," Jean replied. "Americans."

"Ah! Bon!" He mussed Jack's hair, which could only improve it, and gave him the patented big Polynesian man smile.

The Taputus carefully transferred the life raft into the larger boat, where Jean and the kids were also seated. The younger Taputu boys would ride in the dinghy. The little outboard motor repeatedly backfired but would not start. The older boy at the pull cord let it rest for a moment. "Inondées" (flooded), he murmered.

Jean leaned through the door of the life raft. My flesh was a darker gray now. She kept feeling my breath to see if it was there. I could be dead or alive.

"John," she whispered. "They've found us. We're going to the doctor." She squeezed my hand. I heard her, as I had heard the flipping of the motor, and I squeezed back as much as I could. She felt it. Good, I thought, I'm going to the doctor. She got me an appointment. That's good. I just had to let go of the *time* of that appointment.

"Please," Jean said to Papa Taputo, "Can you make the boat go; my husband is almost dead."

Camille, tight beside her, heard this news and began to cry quietly. Jack was more stoic, staring across the coral to the distant wreckage.

The father nodded and the boy spun the motor again. It stuttered, faltered, backfired, and then came to life. We slowly headed into the breeze now across the lagoon. I could feel it; it was good. In the distance, the coconut palms still seemed very far away to Jean. Then, finally, there was a little rooftop visible under the palms, and then another.

"Ma maison!" Papa Taputu pointed to the rusty shacks.

"Very nice," Jean said. She was looking for the little hospital or the doctor or something.

Papa Taputu, after silently pointing back to me with a jerk of his head, looked at Jean squarely and then made a sawing motion with his hand against his own stout leg. He lifted his eyebrows to open the subject.

"No, Monsieur!" she replied. She could see that he was prepared to do it himself as soon as we reached the sand but wanted her to sign the unwritten release.

"Un docteur," she explained. He nodded that he understood, but seemed to think all that might come too late. He was used to solving problems himself.

I wanted to say something. Jean saw it in my eyes and came near. I told her I was going to rest for a while. She said I must not. Absolutely must fight the urge to sleep.

"John, look at me. Stay awake. We're almost…I don't know. We're almost somewhere."

There were so many times in the past sixteen hours when the kids and Jean had so impressed me with their strength, and this strength had infused me, giving me the will to survive. That is no exaggeration. This was like that. I nodded to her that I would keep at it. The pain was just impossible. Unbelievable. It was wearing me out. So I went somewhere else, but I honestly didn't want to get in trouble with Jean.

[8]

AN ISLAND HOME

As the boats pulled up to the little beach near the Taputu's family compound, the sandy isle was not much changed from what Captain Pond first saw. Of course, for them, there was no sign of any past or present human habitation, no family running up to meet them—no welcoming mother in a colorful sarong and no laughing, running little children, which is what we experienced.

The compound, as we entered it, included three corrugated-metal huts raised on stilts over the lip of the lagoon. The stilts were cement-filled oil drums, with much of the metal rusted away, leaving the cement pillars. One of the huts was half over the lagoon and another was entirely over it, with a long gangplank over the water to the front door. The sides of the huts were of rusty, corrugated metal, with some walls thatched. Large, open windows, which could flap down for a storm, overlooked the lagoon.

Their palm-thatched roofs were braced against the wind by outer layers of old fishing net, which draped down from the eaves. A central canopy shaded a long plank table for eating. Fish was drying on a line, and a large pile of coconut husks surrounded a little clearing where some sharp stones lay for that work. A rusty cement pillar with a small satellite dish on it was a ways out in the lagoon. A wire looped from the dish, across the water to the largest hut, which also had a tall radio antenna sticking up through the thatch.

The little Taputu girls were grinning, obviously pleased to see Jack and Camille—certainly the first such visitors. The mother came forward and put her arms around Jean. She was a substantial and quite beautiful woman, also in blues and greens like Papa, her husband. An orange tie in her ponytail matched the orange flowers printed on her blue skirt, and big gold earrings helped light up her face.

"Je suis Diane," she said. "Diane Taputu."

Jean was dizzy. *Where is the doctor?*

The men from the boat carried me, life raft and all, to the shade ramada. Only then did Diane see the problem. She held her hands to her mouth and then, tears in her eyes, came to hold Jean again.

She then went for some clothing. An orange T-shirt for Jean and a print sarong and sandals. Dry shorts and shirts for the kids.

Jean heard Papa Taputu inside the big hut on a radio telephone call. She ducked inside to see Papa working the large, old radio that looked like war surplus. The conversation was in French; he handed the microphone to Jean.

"Madame Silverwood," the man from Mahina Coastal Radio said in blessed English. "What is your situation?"

"My husband is *dying.* His leg was almost cut off, and he lost blood all night."

"Thank you," the calm voice replied. "I understand."

"He is close to death. We really need medical help right *now.*"

"I understand," he repeated. "A rescue helicopter with a doctor will reach you at two ... *dans l'après-midi.*"

Two in the afternoon? That was four hours away.

"My husband will die."

"Madame, we will do our very best to have the helicopter reach you as soon as possible."

In the raft, I was staring up at where I was, the deep blue sky. When she returned from the radio hut, Jean folded a palm frond into a fan and whisked the flies away from my leg.

"*Viens,*" Diane said. "Mange un peu" (eat something), she said as she laid out *poisson cru* and *crêpes* on the table, along with coconut milk and plastic mugs of coffee sweetened with condensed milk. Jean and the kids were not hungry, but they picked at it to be polite, and because they knew they needed it.

Diane then gave the pearl-and-gold jewelry to Camille, Amelia, and Jean. The pearl meant something very special to Jean; it meant somehow things would be okay.

Just the same, after about forty minutes with still no helicopter, Jean had Papa Taputu call Coastal Radio Mahina again. The same man advised her that the helicopter had refueled in Bora-Bora and was en route.

The little Taputu girls helped Camille climb up into their hut. They brought out two tabby kittens. She petted the kittens mechanically and stared, her eyes dead and expressionless.

Almost noon, and still no sign of the helicopter. Jean insisted Papa call again. The radio voice assured her that the helicopter was on its way with a doctor, a diver, and a nurse. With Amelia now brushing the flies from my leg, Jean paced along the water's edge, staring down the horizon until it would please produce a helicopter, which of course it did.

The thump of rotors sounded across the lagoon from the east. Jean was sobbing to see the great blue-and-white machine draw near; she was clinging tightly now to Ben, her face buried in his shoulder. He told her it was going to be okay now. The helicopter made a wide turn over the length of the little island.

———

What took less than a minute for the copter had taken Captain Pond a very long day to explore. We were so close to rescue now; Pond's ordeal did not have the benefit of our technological advantages.

After searching for water all day, Captain Pond returned to the stranded people on the reef around 4:00 p.m with good and bad news. No village, no water yet, but dry land where they might survive.

He had earlier instructed the ship's carpenter and the other crew members left on the reef to begin work on a raft while he was on his recon mission. With timbers, spars, and heavy rope, they had constructed a large raft during the day, a project that raised the spirits of those building and those watching.

Despite that, it was not an entirely wonderful day, as Miss Spangenberg reported:

> We remained in the water all that day, keeping as close as possible to prevent the sharks from attacking us, as there were a great many of them swimming about close to us. We had nothing to eat all day, and truly presented a miserable group; almost naked, our faces bloated, and our lips swollen to an unusual size.

How can I not think of Amelia, standing all night and all morning in those same blood-tinted waters to hold the raft, watching for the sharks that were surely there—the grandchildren, by many generations, of the same sharks that so worried young Esther. Every new wave knocks you off your perch a bit; you are constantly struggling to keep from getting lacerated, either by coral or worse. The coral is so sharp that the beach flip-flops the kids were wearing were cut through by the blades of the reef. A box cutter could not have cut cleaner.

As evening approached, Pond directed Mr. Coffin to move all the women and children, and as many of their husbands and fathers as could be managed, to the island via the small boat. Once they were there, the accommodations were hardly five-star, but they were a great improvement over standing in the shark-infested reef. This night they would sleep, or try to, on hard rocks under a cold wind. Esther reported that it was a "wretched night lying on bare rock."

Let me pause to testify regarding the wretchedness of the bare rocks in what I presume is that very spot. As the helicopter landed out on a coral shelf on the seaward side, French medics ran to my raft and were soon crouched inside with me. They began a plasma IV and a hundred other things. They dressed the wound, which was impossible, of course. They were constantly on the radio with a physician and the sound of all this was rather dire. I didn't like the near-panic in their voices; nor did Jean. She was getting it that they thought I was not going to make it.

She realized she would need to rehearse in her own mind how to break it to the kids, if these medics suddenly turned to her and shook their heads, covering my face with a soggy jacket. What would she do? She looked around for the kids. Camille was walking along the lagoon's edge with the island children, watching hundreds of baby turtles swimming in the shallows. Jack was sitting near the water, looking glum. I don't know if he was depressed about me or about Speedy the turtle.

Maybe things had worked out for Speedy. We had, as a matter of remarkable fact, crashed into a recognized turtle sanctuary. His landlubber ways were perhaps unfamiliar to this variety of sea turtle, but, who knows? Maybe they would welcome him as some kind of god. One could hope. I'm sure Jack was thinking all sorts of possible outcomes for Speedy. But his big worry was probably me.

Jean looked at her children and tried to summon that feeling of utter peace she had experienced on the bow. That would be the right mental place to be if she had to break the news. She remembered when we dove with scuba tanks deep along a reef in Rangiroa, between the Marquesas and Tahiti. That was, she now realized, the perfect moment that this trip had been all about. She needed to get her mind back there now.

Such a high and frightening sea it had been, just before the dive. We were taken out of the Rangiroa lagoon through a channel into the deep sea. The incoming tide met the wind and the still-exiting water from the last cycle of the lagoon in a way that made the waves swell to twelve feet. As the waves approached the boat they looked like they would topple upon us, and Jean screamed. The Frenchman looked at her as if she was crazy, but we had never been on a dive like this before and I have to admit it was intimidating. A Polynesian man, about twenty, was piloting the rubber powerboat—his hot rod—out through the waves.

"Put on the masks and the fins," the dive master, a bald, muscular Frenchman, shouted to us over the roar of the sea and the outboard engine.

Poor Amelia was petrified. She does not like that thing where you flip backward into the water from a boat—she would rather slip in feetfirst. And this sea was like a whitewater-rapids trip where you think you cannot stay on the boat another ten seconds. She squeezed my hand and said, "Daddy, I'm too scared. I really can't do this."

"Put een your mouthpieces, s'il vous plait."

"Really, Daddy; I can't be here."

"Allez! Allez! Now! We go!"

She closed her eyes, clutched tighter to my hand, and rolled backward over the wide rubber side. We all rolled into the furious sea together. Jack and Camille were too young to dive, and so were playing on the beach with the dive master's wife, eating ice cream and being watched; but Jean and Ben and Amelia and I, we went in.

Once you go down, the fury of the sea ends in an instant. It is shockingly peaceful. You look up as you descend, and you see the wildly dancing prisms of the waves above, but they are of that world, not this one below. You descend. I looked at Amelia, and she was all right. Huge smile. Everything was okay now.

The water was crystal. The steep cliff of the coral reef was before us as we descended along its pillars and caves. Coral fans and sea life of every color waved in the tidal breeze. Sunlight in ever-shifting columns roamed over us and into the distance. In the deep blue beyond, as the reef descended its mile to the ocean floor, these glittering sea beams illuminated distant reef sharks in schools, and larger sharks moving majestically in the greater distance. The silence is at first eerie as you watch yourself and your family decend and drift in slow motion deeper toward the ocean floor. Then a sound. A magical sound, over and over again. The song of the whale.

Amelia and I were diving buddies. Jean was diving with Ben, which pretty much meant she was diving alone; Ben is always off exploring, leaving you behind, but the dive master stayed close to us for backup.

I had been so mad at Ben back in the Caribbean when we went for the big dive that certified him, Jean, Amelia, and myself as scuba divers. There was a shipwreck in the area that the dive instructor told us to avoid. Shipwrecks can be deadly to inexperienced divers. You lose track of time, or you get stuck, or you cut a hose on an old piece of rusty metal. Too much can go wrong around a shipwreck.

So, I look around and can't find Ben. There he is over at the wreck. He is swimming through it, into one big hole in its deck and out the other, looping around, upside down, backward, doing barrel rolls, in and out like a stunt flier through a barn.

When we got to the surface, I was sure the instructor would give him a good yelling and refuse to certify him. He didn't mention it. I was so mad that I did. I asked the instructor if he had seen Ben on the wreck.

The man looked at me seriously.

"I did," he said. "Ben is a natural diver."

So, sometimes parenting is like that: You are dead wrong. You learn Everybody is a genius at some things, and they are going to do those things and that's the way it is.

So I kept an extra eye on Jean because I knew Ben would be in the caves, around the far side of anything that had a far side, and I would say to myself that Ben is a natural diver.

I do not mean to suggest that he is foolhardy—far from it. He just really knows what he is doing. Same with surfing. When, in Tahiti, we visited Teahupoo, home to world-class surfers and competitions, he saw waves bigger than our house. And he just told me that he wasn't experienced enough for the heaviest waves in the world—and he was plenty experienced. He has a professional eye for that sort of thing—for his limits. So I had seen that and learned that about him. He didn't need as much parenting as I thought, or he had matured a lot. Both.

I cannot describe the beauty of that dive in Rangiroa. It was called a drift dive, because you just ride with the tide as it is sucked into the lagoon and gives you a free ride past the wall of the reef.

We were over a hundred feet down, and the life around us was extraordinary. There are about five hundred varieties of coral—every color, shape, and texture, and about sixteen hundred kinds of fish. Moray eels poked their long heads out of lairs in the reef and looked at us as we passed. Schools of reef sharks swam below. Delicate, white-laced sea anemones, deadly to the touch but elixir to the eye, waved in the currents and made homes for the colorful clown fish, who, alone in the world, are immune to the anemone toxin and live among them in a cooperative arrangement.

Huge rays swam in the distance. Size is very difficult to judge underwater, as is distance, because the temperature gradient of the water— colder with each meter of depth—creates a great lens of distortion. Even so, the great manta rays must have been half the size of our boat. Then schools of silver tuna, emperor fish, big grouper, tiny neon-colored fish around us like confetti in Times Square.

The dive master summoned Amelia to his side. He held her arm and took her lower. He handed her a frond of soft coral and introduced her to a giant sea turtle that had a shell as big as a camping tent. It hovered near, its head and fins mottled with a white web pattern over black. With fins poised, beak and eyes prominent, it looked like a great bird in its glide. She fed the lovely beast, whose head was the size of hers and who looked in her big eyes with his big eyes as he munched. She was thirteen at the time; he was well over one hundred. But it was love at first sight for them both.

I glanced around to find Jean. She was nearby, watching. We looked at each other and shook our heads. This was it. This was exactly it.

But the memory of that perfect moment did not give her any peace now. She was not interested in merging with nature, accepting mortality. She decided she just would not be able to do a good job of telling the kids that I hadn't made it, so she decided to not let me die. That's the only way she could figure how to get through the day.

She came close. I squeezed her hand. She looked into my eyes and understood that I wanted to say something, but hardly had the strength. She drew nearer so I might just barely whisper.

"The damn flies," I said. "Get rid of the damn flies," and I let her hand go.

I motioned for her again, and again she leaned to my lips.

"How do these people live with these damned flies," I said.

"Shh, John! They'll hear you," she said.

I was pretty crazy. I was thinking it was a little more comfortable back on the reef. No flies. Softer to be floating there, instead of lying on this rocky beach.

Yves Peltrault, the helicopter copilot, hunkered down beside me. He grasped my hand.

"So, John," he said, "we are going to get you and your family out of here, okay?"

"Where's Jack?" I croaked. "I don't know what reef we hit. The sea was huge coming in behind us, it crushed our boat. Ben and I had the raft on deck, but ... the whole boat, it flooded so fast. My kids were screaming, you know?" I was more than a little out of it.

Yves slowed me down, calmed me down. He leaned closer and spoke slowly. "It's okay. It's okay. You are here now, John, and we are caring for you, you see? Your family is good. All of them. Everyone is okay."

"The mast fell on my leg, it stayed on top of me," I explained through my teeth. "I couldn't save my family. I couldn't move."

"They are okay now," he repeated.

"The pain was … the mast bounced on my leg—kept bouncing on it. It was hard to pray. I couldn't pray right … I couldn't just die and leave them there."

I told Yves to take care of my wife and kids. Then he told me that I was leaving the island in a few minutes with them. That didn't register with me. You see, I had lost all sense of self, didn't see myself in this movie anymore. Yves somehow got that. I heard him say, "John, we are none of us leaving without you, no. Think about your children, John. Do they go on without you? No, absolutely no."

Poor Yves knew they had to get going, and he tried to rev me up for the trip. "You are the strong one, John, the father, don't forget you are to live, you are here with us. Forget your pain, or hate it, yes, but you have survived everything, John, because you are meant to. John, John, know God wants you to live."

I wanted to know if the beacon had worked—if that's why they had come.

Yves smiled. "Yes, John, we come from your signal, the call to the satellite. We are come for you from Papeete in Tahiti, *non?*"

I was starting to lose consciousness. They hurried me aboard the helicopter, with Jean and the kids taking their seats around me. As the rotors lifted us high over the little family huts, they could see the atoll below and, stringing out into the distance, the hard reef that had changed our course as a family. I watched Dr. Volpeliere's face as he spoke, arms locked on both sides of my stretcher, but his voice was lost in the sound of the engines.

Our beautiful *Emerald Jane* was, by now, nearly digested by the reef. She was floating in chips down the long underwater way to the mile-deep ocean floor. She was mixing with some gold coins and bones, as I have said. All that we saved of her was ourselves and the little beacon, which deserved special consideration. The little nest that Ben made for his family on the ledge of the reef probably lasted until the next high tide, and then it, too, filtered into the deep. There is no plaque to mark where Amelia was brave for her father or where Ben grew up to take care of his family. Nothing there for the love of a wife, the suffering of young children.

Of course, it would be mounted next to the far larger plaque of names from 1855, topped by that of Benjamin Franklin Pond, who, as we were heading away from the island after our one long day, was only beginning his stay.

———

After Captain Pond sent the women and children to the island, he stayed on the reef with the men for that second night. Some of the men crowded up onto the new raft, but space there was mostly given to the older and injured. The tide was higher this second night, covering those not on the raft up to their chests. These men were near-dying of thirst.

On the next morning, rather than use the boat to ferry the remaining survivors to the island, Pond instructed Coffin to go on an expedition to find water, while he would lead the men to the island by raft; a second raft had been constructed by this time.

At midmorning, the supplies that had been scavenged from the wreck, including a sealed barrel of bread, some bags of beans, several bags of wet flour, a great many tins of peas, and a great heap of wet clothing, were loaded onto the rafts beside the elder and damaged men. As the lagoon was too difficult a climb over the coral with the rafts and supplies, the company moved through the surf slowly along the reef toward its island portion.

In the deep sections, the shorter men could only hang on to the edge of the raft while the taller searched for toeholds that would allow them to push the rafts along.

Two men nearly drowned when crossing one of the wilder areas. As they left a trail of blood, up to twenty sharks at a time followed them and were beaten away as the men pushed along, exhausted, lacerated, and dying of thirst.

They reached the soil of the island at dusk, in time for the women and children to cheer them and lead them to a fine invention: holes dug in the sand so that water would leak into oyster shells laid down inside, the sand of the island acting to filter the salt of the sea.

The men drank carefully from the little shells, but all they wanted, and they grinned, with great, blistered smiles.

A large flour barrel would later be buried to its rim and serve as a constant well. Warming fires would burn beginning the day after the group was reunited, as a sailor produced a magnifying glass from his pocket and used the sun to ignite some shredded-palm kindling. The first cooked meal was oysters—the island is home to great oyster beds.

Pond organized the men, declaring that they may be on the island for some time, and would need hunting parties, lookouts, fishermen, and builders. He insisted that any food so obtained should be given to a common kitchen for the feeding of all. It was agreed. He had earned their respect at every turn, and would not be refused now. He had passed his test.

> We divided ourselves into families, built huts, and thatched them with the leaves of the pandanus tree. All the provisions found were thrown into one common stock, and equally divided among each mess every morning, and we gradually became reconciled to our sad fate.
>
> —Pond

With the basic organizing accomplished, Pond led a party to explore the remainder of the reef. Another spit of land was found, containing about twenty coconut trees. This food would greatly increase their chance of survival. Pond positioned one of the men on the island with a signal fire that faced a different direction from the main camp, and might be sighted by a passing ship that would not see the other beach. At no moment, it seems, was Mr. Pond not thinking clearly.

After the easily found oysters were exhausted, sand crabs and some small turtles made their way into the coconut soup of the island. It was discovered that, if the ladies' hunting party went to the beaches at midnight, turtles could be found coming to beach to lay their eggs. A three-hundred-pound sea turtle was lassoed by the excited women and later sacrificed to the fire. Young boys were recruited in the days following to go out at night, look for turtles, turn them on their backs, and return to their huts. The creatures were dispatched in the morning by the women, or put in pens alive where they could be kept until needed. Turtle pancakes, made with the eggs of the sea creatures, grated coconut, and some flour, was a specialty on the children's menu.

Sharks, ever patrolling close to the beach, were caught by literal hook and crook and added to the survivors' diet.

Seeds were saved from some of the foods, but all attempts at gardening were short-lived.

The days had stretched into weeks and then into a second month.

Evening fires and singing provided some sense of home, but there was a desperate feeling to the camp, a constant eye to the horizon, and a ready signal fire. The thought that people back home must be suffering to think them dead weighed heavily on all.

Captain Pond was seen some days and nights taking his measure of the sky with the quadrant. He concluded they were three- to five-hundred miles from the nearest settlement within the Society Islands. He also concluded that the wreck had been caused by a sixteen-mile error in the charts. I do not know if the charts were those of Wallis or Bligh, or of another.

It was becoming clear in the second month that they would have to rescue themselves. Daily trips to the wreck were made to salvage the bits necessary to make the quarter boat into a seaworthy vessel for sailing with a small mast and sail, and also for two-abreast, ten-man rowing. The carpenter made a blacksmith's forge at the camp to make the necessary nails and fittings. Sail canvas and broken door panels became the bellows of the forge.

[9]

ESCAPE PLANS

The trade winds were consistently blowing now from the nearest islands, 250 miles away, not toward them. The islands downwind, the Navigator Islands—now called the Somoon Islands—were some 1,500 miles away, but, given the wind, seemed to be the only possibility. Coffin, a great seaman, agreed. After all, Bligh had navigated twice such a distance in a small boat. Yes, but this did seem to Pond almost like suicide. He nevertheless felt obliged to try. He picked his four best seamen and a date was set for departure. The quarter boat, floating at anchor in the lagoon near camp, was loaded with the navigation items and a supply of food for a long journey.

Pond sent men out to find an outlet to the sea from the lagoon, for atoll reefs nearly always have one or more main channels. None could be found during the first two days searching—it seemed that the sea just came and went through the teeth of the coral, not through any channels. This news caused a deep despair in the camp. Carrying the boat directly over the reef into the surf would destroy the boat—an inlet was needed.

Finally, an area was discovered that would do, though there would be reasonable difficulty getting the boat over some shallows. The departure was set for the following day.

The near-futility of the coming journey, and the idea that he was abandoning the community on the island, sent Pond into a depression. He understood that if he had made the wrong decision, the people might never be saved. There is nothing quite like that feeling—the feeling that, as captain, you have failed to protect those in your care, and that they might die on account of your error or weakness.

His mood was taken up by the weather, which turned wild and purple that evening and pressed down upon him further. Late that night, a tropical storm broke across the island with great violence. Pond, unable to sleep, went down to the beach of the lagoon, fighting the wind and rain, to check on the boat. It was gone—ripped from its anchorage. The navigation equipment and the stores for the trip had all been placed aboard. Nearly all the useful scraps that could be recovered from the *Julia Ann*, and had been molded or blacksmithed into the features and fittings of the quarter boat, were now also gone.

Leaving supplies on the boat during the storm and not securing the boat more surely indicate that Pond was no longer quite on his game; he was making mistakes.

The crew and passengers gathered on the beach in the predawn hour. They were completely distraught over the loss of what they thought must be their one chance to ever be saved.

Pond recovered his good instincts and his leadership spirit, which must always be positive. My captain Ben maintained he would get me out, and Pond declared that their boat was probably not sunk; its canvas cover had probably saved it from being swamped. It had most likely just dragged its anchor across the lagoon to one of the smaller islands and was now there waiting. A party was dispatched and they in fact found it. It was nearly sunk, so filled had it become with water, but it was otherwise undamaged, as were the goods and supplies inside. The bad news was that now Pond would have to take the trip.

At this time one of the missionaries, thought to be John McCarthy, had a vivid dream of the little boat adrift upside down in the sea and the bodies of the men floating near it. The tale of this dream spread through the camp, and the men who had volunteered to go suddenly changed their minds.

Pond may have been secretly pleased by the outcome, but, to prevent the rise of a priestly governance, he ordered that "there should be no more visions told in public unless favorable ones, and first submitted to me for my approval."

Pond changed his plans: He ordered the boat fitted for ten oarsmen. It would head east instead, into the wind, to the closer Society Islands.

The same dreamer reported to Pond in private that he had dreamed favorably on the plan. Pond asked him if he believed his dreams. He did. Then he would not mind coming as an oarsman? The man was recruited.

Coffin, who had spent half his life in great and small whaling boats, instantly opposed the wild idea. It was madness, rowing against the wind so far, so low in the water. How even to feed ten men? It was sure death for those men, Coffin argued angrily, and it would be slow death for those remaining on the island, who would never be rescued and would die of scurvy and whatever misfortunes and diseases befall castaways.

Pond was greatly uneasy to have Coffin on the other side of the argument, but he insisted.

The needed oarsmen volunteered, and the boat was modified for their coming labors, which would be Herculean whether they succeeded or died trying. When the passengers objected to Pond leaving them, he faltered a moment, until the oarsmen said they would not go without him. That settled it for Pond, and for the community at large, who agreed that Pond had led them well before, and that he would and could do this great thing and return to rescue them. They mustered their spirits to give the men a hearty send-off. Only Coffin remained mute.

On December 3, a few days before the planned departure, Second Mate Owens ran into the captain's hut to wake him. There was some news. The captain struggled awake to take it in. The winds had changed; they could sail east instead of rowing. They must leave immediately. Pond gave the order and gathered his own things for the journey. He walked down to the beach where the other men were ready at the boat. Two casks of water were aboard—not much. They also had jerked turtle meat and some salt pork saved from the wreck. No more supplies could be stowed, and the boat was already inches from swamping with all ten men aboard. Coffin was right that it was madness and foolhardy desperation. The suggestion had been made that all the rowers might not be needed now that the boat had the wind, but Pond, knowing the future or at least the vagaries of Pacific weather, insisted that they would be needed.

The castaways of the island ran along the seaward beach as the quarter boat rowed through the shallows and bucked over the breakers, making it into the open sea and hoisting a sail to a great cheer from the beach. Pond had the helm and turned the tiller to his planned course.

The ten men sailed for three days and two nights with a good quartering wind. As Pond had feared, the wind then shifted and they were left to begin rowing—sailing by "ash breeze," as the old sailors called it, because oars were commonly made of strong but light ash wood. As they rowed, they watched storm clouds rise in the distance, and the sea became broken and then choppy.

This, I must note, is the exact route we took away from the island as we sped overhead in the helicopter. Jean looked at me on the stretcher and at one point was sure I had died. But I was in good hands and staying inside myself, as were the men under the command of Pond.

They rowed onward to Pond's exhortations into the eyes of the storm. When the boat was near swamping from the waves, and when the men were too exhausted to give the boat the power it needed to steer up and down the waves without disaster, they tied canvas over it as snug as they could manage, and lay under it, letting the storm have them like a cork. For long hours, they knew that at any minute a wave might tip them or come down too hard on the canvas and they would be gone. The men prayed under the canvas and hoped for deliverance or at least for luck.

As the storm began to pass after several hours, a mate peeked out from under the canvas into the now-shining afternoon sun. "Land!" he cried out.

The storm had borne them to the waters off Bora-Bora, a suitably inhabited destination. They peeled off their covering and rowed with restored energy. But the wind and sea took them farther from, not closer to, the island. It began to disappear on the horizon. Pond led the men to keep rowing, stronger and faster, until they were nearly dying of exhaustion; if they didn't make Bora-Bora, they'd die anyway. The dot reappeared on the horizon. They drew closer with each hour of painful exertion. Their water was spent. Finally they were searching for a way into the reef surrounding the island. A native fisherman on the reef waved and pointed the way.

Likewise, our Navy chopper had touched down on Bora-Bora. They were low on fuel, and had radioed ahead requesting the Guardian aircraft be made ready to haul me the final leg to Tahiti, and the hospital. Once lifted through the bomb bay, four tense sets of eyes stayed with me for a tense six-hundred-mile-per-hour emergency blast into Papeete. We covered in exactly twenty-two minutes a distance that had taken Pond's men twenty-four hours.

They had done it. The schooner *Emma Packer* would soon be on its way to the atoll reef of Scilly Island, with Pond aboard and waving from the deck to the torch-fire celebration on the evening shore. It was their sixtieth day on the island. They sailed to Tahiti the next day, like my family flew, shoeless, in tattered rags, and as brown-skinned as the beautiful Tahitians.

[10]

THE REEF BACK HOME

Happy endings do not usually come clean-cut. The survivors of the *Julia Ann*, our sister ship, as I have called it, struggled for months more to make their ways to America, enduring hunger and rude officials; Pond was even held as a prisoner until he could guarantee the passage of those stranded in Tahiti. And my own trip home had its bumps, as my hospital stay was not without its scares, and my later accommodation to my new condition came slowly.

But we did go home. When we arrived to check into the Air Tahiti desk, we were stunned to see most of the French officers who had rescued us lined up with their wives, husbands, and children. They all wore and held beautiful shell leis for us, in the Polynesian tradition. I have been in touch with them a great deal, and have sailed with one of them since.

I must not leave our brother Pond in the Tahiti jail. He was released to arrange passage for the remnants of his passengers who were having difficulty getting to California. Then he disembarked for Panama. This was not his first fortune lost, as he had begun his career as a gold miner and was used to the ups and downs of life. He would move on to other business adventures and travels and would do all right. I'm hoping I can, too.

I do wonder what he did in Panama. That was long before T.R. built the canal there, of course, so it would have been a very different place from what we saw. I will remember it as one of the great and literal passages of our journey and of my life.

I expect Pond went to Panama City, which is on the Pacific side of the narrow nation. It must then have been a wild and erotic place of danger and opportunity. It is now a big city not unlike so many others.

Colón, the city on the Caribbean side of Panama, must today be more like what Pond experienced. Ben and I had some guy-time there, and we would have been happy to run into Pond and have a steak with him. We could have shared some warnings of the dangerous waters behind Pond and ahead of us. That steak would have been $3.50 at the yacht club in Colón, by the way—today's prices.

Of course, the club there is maybe not what you would expect, if you think the sailing life is pretty fancy. It really isn't, and the yacht club in Colón is perhaps the central argument in that case. The main room has some old chairs and tables like those in a school cafeteria in a poor country. A lady there will do your ship's laundry for a few dollars. Her husband will help you pull your broken generator. He will be gone most of the day, for quite a few days, looking for parts and not finding them in town. Your wife will abandon you, as the place is a fly-infested steam bath and there is no power on the boat now for the air-conditioning. She will go to a tourist hotel with the kids.

Ben stayed with me on the boat, and we kept at the repairs and paperwork for two weeks.

You do not just sail up to the locks of the Panama Canal, reach over, and knock. It takes a great deal of paperwork. I suppose the shipping companies have it all rigged and ready for their arrival, but we sailboaters often have to wait a long time for things to be approved. We had a rugged old Brit name Pete, who looked like he had been down there a while, as our fixer, our agent. He got it all done, but it took a long time. Pete introduced us to Carlos, who had a cab. You don't just go out on the street and hail a cab. You want to know the guy. You don't want to end up in the jungle, robbed and dead. Carlos was good and taught us about the town. The danger of the place did not stop Jean and Carolyne from taking their morning run, however. They ran where and when Carlos told them they would be "pretty safe"—good enough for Jean, who seriously needs her run and will take a risk for it. "Early mornings are safe nearly everywhere, as criminals tend to sleep late," he said.

Ben met an Australian girl in Colón. She was a few years older than he. Long, blond hair; good-looking girl. Her name was Bridget. She invited him on their boat to watch a movie about two characters named Ben and Bridget, *Forces of Nature*, maybe. He might have been a bit interested in her. She learned his age and that was a problem for her. Silly girl. But it is a steamy part of the world and a good place to feel the forces of nature. Continents and hemispheres are organisms in a way, with their own areas of specialty—brainy and otherwise; and if Florida is one suggestive part of the Americas, Panama is certainly another.

I took some walks around the city and had time to myself to think about who I was and where I was in my life. I had just come off that tough time drinking in the Caribbean, so here was a good place to look at life and all its temptations and directions and decide on the upper road or the lower. The Guajira storm was my fork in the road. There are a lot of forces playing on us, whether known to you or not, always are, but sometimes you just need to decide who you're going to be.

Walking past the boats, big and small, fancy and dilapidated, I realized how I had been captive to boats since childhood—since ninth grade, really, when I helped clean and repaint iron ingots of ballast for a boat belonging to the father of a boy who would become my lifelong friend Penn Coffey.

Penn's father started taking us out on the water. We would cruise Chesapeake Bay and explore way up its rivers. The captain would spot an unguarded cornfield here and there and mention that the corn looked pretty ripe. That was an order to swim ashore and bring back some lunch or dinner. It was a life of freedom and beauty that stuck with me. My own dad is a great guy, too, more the rocket scientist who has always had high expectations for his boys—and we really feel that. But the water, the boats, beauty and a simple breeze; I was so hooked.

———

With the new power generator on the boat, we were finally ready to go up through that tight passage to the great Pacific, thanking Teddy Roosevelt for the shortcut. Ben was changing, too. We would have more blowups, but I could see the man in him coming forward, even as I regretted his former reliance on me departing.

Jean had a similar experience with Amelia on the Pacific side of Panama. Amelia is a fine dancer, but one of her secret loves is horseback riding. I say "secret" because she does not talk about it much. We really aren't set up to have horses—takes a huge amount of money to do it right. I think she doesn't talk about it because she doesn't want to pressure me to get horses. She's a sensitive kid. But our California hills are pretty horsey, and she had spent plenty of time riding with her friends. In Panama, she dusted off her riding boots and found a riding club were she could ride and jump about three times a week for the time we were there. Sometimes she took a trusted cab by herself, but often Jean would go along just to watch her. Looking across the field at this young woman riding so beautifully was a real moment for Jean. We had both come on this trip to find our old selves. It seems we had reproduced.

If it was time for us to move on from who we had been, Jean got a boost at a hotel beauty shop in Panama. They misunderstood whatever it was she said and dyed her hair red. Unfortunately, it had changed back to blond by the time she had that great orange T-shirt in the Tahiti hospital. The beauty accident was a blessing in disguise, as people treated her completely differently on the Panamanian streets. When she was a blonde, they always assumed she was an American tourist. When she was a redhead, they talked to her as if she were a local. She liked that.

I guess it was interesting for me, too. Jean and I have always gotten along pretty well in the sack, if you don't mind my mentioning it. I can't look at her without wanting her. I think I had some fantasy ideas about this voyage: secluded beaches, the boat to ourselves some afternoons, anchored in some lagoon. Me and Jean.

There were times, of course—the drinking thing—when I was glad for that couch out in the cockpit; Jean didn't even want me on her planet, much less her pillow. But, as Bishop Fulton J. Sheen once said as he came onstage for the *Ed Sullivan Show* and was looking into the wings at the chorus girls still exiting from the previous act, "Just because you're on a diet doesn't mean you can't look at the menu," I still looked at her when she was going for a swim or a run, or was walking around the salon or, you know, breathing.

And, frankly, we had always used intimacy as a way to get past arguments. Having real time together is never easy in a family of four kids, especially on a boat, but humans are very good at figuring things out. Hey, it was difficult even when there was one kid in the house. When Ben was a toddler, we even hid in a closet once. On the voyage, sometimes we would take the dinghy out and find a secluded beach. If the Van Zwams were in port with us, sometimes we would take their kids for an afternoon and they would reciprocate.

And sometimes we could do some necking up on deck when the kids were asleep or busy down below. In the South Pacific, anchored in Huahine, we leaned against the mast together, watched the stars, and listened to the Polynesian music echoing across the water from the village. Jack, Camille, and Amelia were sleeping, and Ben was reading a book. Just to hold Jean is always pretty good medicine for me. Ben's stateroom was right under us, so we kept it G-rated. Maybe R.

On Water Island back near Saint Thomas, we walked on a very secluded beach. The view was unbelievable. This was when I was still in trouble with Jean for the drinking, but we were both thinking it was time to move on. I kissed the girl, and we found a place between the palm trees to relax. At one point, Jean glanced over to see a large land tortoise staring at her. I think she got a wink. The kids were babysitting themselves; we could see the boat out across the harbor. We had even called the pizza boat—there are such things in the wild world—and we saw it arriving and knew we had more time. There was a warm tropical breeze. Finally a light rain sent us home, happy as clams.

Sometimes our dinghy has been seen out at anchor with no one visible in it. Sometimes it is rocking with the waves, sometimes more.

We can get pretty angry, and, you know, no one ever wins an argument in a marriage, so you need ways to get over it, and we have always managed. And the change in my body wasn't a problem. If you are newly an amputee, I won't tell you that chicks dig it, but it really isn't a problem. It's all about attitude and love, and enthusiasm for *them*. I have always been so enthusiastic about Jean. I remember seeing her through binoculars somewhere. She was on the beach with the kids, and I was out on the boat. She was the only woman on the beach I wanted to look at. It could even have been Orient Beach. We had that honeymoon in Ireland that I can't get out of my mind. Wouldn't want to.

After the hospital time in Tahiti, we didn't go back to Panama chasing Pond's ghost; we parted company with that grand fellow and went our own way home to golden California. Maybe I'll look him up in the next life. After my second amputation, I had a fevered conversation with him, explaining what happened to us. In doing so, I think I figured out what happened. When we were dead in the water trying to fix the broken boom bracket, I think we drifted farther than we realized, and somehow our electronic compass was not working with the autopilot. While we were on the correct compass heading, we didn't know the current was moving us laterally to starboard. On the other hand, it might have been Fletcher

Christian's fault—it might have been a crummy map. I guess it doesn't matter now, except for the storytelling.

At home, after a hard year. I spent some time feeling sorry for myself and thinking I was a freak. It came to a breaking point, and I had to decide to just let it go. Kinda like accepting pain when there's no other choice. "Fisherman's reef" is the way I thought of it. Not the coral or rock kind of reef, but when you reef the sail, meaning you take it in a little because the wind is too strong. But sometimes it is even too strong to take it down a reef, and then you are in trouble unless you know how to do what they call the fisherman's reef.

I learned it when we were first bringing the *Emerald Jane* up to New York from Florida. I had a good sailor at the helm to show me how to sail a big cat. We hit Tropical Storm Bill, which sure felt like a hurricane to me. And it came on fast.

At about 10:30 that morning, we cast off from the Palm Beach marina and steered eastward to catch the Gulf Stream. We knew the storm was coming, but there had been a break in the weather and we thought we could outrun the next piece of it.

I called Jean on my cell phone—she and the kids were in California. It was early morning there.

"The break in the weather's holding," I told her, "so we're finally on our way."

"I wish I were with you," she said. In a little while, I would wonder if that had maybe been our last conversation.

In the light northerly breeze, the big cat averaged only four and a half knots. But that speed, added to the steady flow of the Gulf Stream current, gave us over six knots. We planned to make the first stop in Beaufort, North Carolina, for a breather before tackling notoriously stormy Cape Hatteras.

The next morning before dawn, the landward horizon was sparking up pretty good with lightning; black squall lines swept to the north and south of us. The sea was getting lumpy, with hard gusts blowing off the waves. We shut down the autopilot and I took the wheel while Glenn, the cat sailor, went into the salon to download a forecast update on the weather fax.

"Too much lightning static," he said, returning to the wheel and managing to light yet another of his constant cigarettes.

"All garbled. But this feels like the makings of a dang hurricane. The glass is droppin' too."

As the wind swung farther south, the Gulf Stream sea humped up in white-crested ridges ten feet high. They tossed the boat about violently. I watched the gusts on the wind-speed indicator: thirty knots and rising. I realized we were carrying way too much sail.

Glenn did not seem too concerned. Still puffing away with the thing stuck in the corner of his mouth, he eased the boat a little into the east as the wind increased.

"The harder Thee blows," Glenn sang, "the faster she goes!"

He launched into a sea shanty from his endless mental jukebox:

"Way, haul away, we'll haul for better weather! Way, haul away, boys! we'll haul away together!"

Then he went to the wilder shanties: "Well, first I (diddled) an Irish girl, her name was Kitty Brinnigan..."

He held the wheel and reached behind to slacken the mainsheet as he swung fast to starboard.

"Ease the jib!" he yelled. I followed his orders as he worked the gale and the boat together through the day and night.

The following morning, I spotted an ominous, greenish squall line sweeping toward us.

"We gotta reef the main," I shouted over the storm to Glenn. It was my boat now, and I didn't want to lose her on her first trip. The bimini awning puffed up like a blowfish.

Glenn threw away his cigarette and slacked the mainsheet, which is controlled by the line wrapped around the big chrome windlass behind him. He then turned the boat almost completely downwind and gave the wheel to Penn Coffey. The rain was horizontal and it stung hard when it hit you; balls of spindrift sea foam sailed by like monster snowflakes.

Reefing, as I think you know, requires hauling down the big sail until it is short enough to work with the wind. Too much sail and you'll lose a mast, flip over in the storm, or head nose-first into a wave and flip head-first. We figured we'd take the sail down two reef points, which are the re-inforced ribs in the sail. You know this.

"But we're going *downwind*," I protested as we headed for the main mast. I had always, always, been taught never to reef a sail downwind.

"We're dickin' around here," Glenn shouted. "Just do what I tell you, bud, and watch me!"

"First, snug yer toppin' lift right up hard," he said, turning the winch. "I'll slack the main halyard while you crank the cringle downhaul . . ." That means something, but I'll spare you.

With the strength of the winches, we managed to haul the big sail down slowly, despite the tons of wind filling it.

But in the time it took to shorten the mainsail to the first reef point, the full brutality of the squall swept in. The wind roared to 65 knots, nudging hurricane strength.

"Forget the second reef!" he shouted. "We gotta ease the main!" He raced back to take the wheel from Penn.

"Okay! Okay! Listen! Slack the main all the way out right *now*!"

With that, I let the line fly around the winch, and the big sail flapped loose like a flag in the wind, having dumped its wind load entirely. Penn turned the boat at a heading that would work for that. He had the squall coming in now off our port beam.

The maneuver had likely saved the ship.

"It's called a fisherman's reef," Glenn said. "When a squall hits too fast to reef the main, it'll keep the mast from blowin' down. Or the boat from flippin' over. Take your pick. You try and run off before the wind with a lot of sail up, you better know the get-out-of-jail cards."

So that's what I did, finally, when the whole amputee thing was too much wind on me. Just let it go loose and fly by. Just loosened up and waited it out and let people love me.

You get love from somebody, from above and from so many some-bodies in my case, and you can pretty much weather anything. And so many people have much, much bigger problems. How lucky I was, how blessed, finally occurred to me while I was driving around the neighbor-hood, practicing driving again. Just then, the thought that the falling mast had come within a whisper of killing Ben struck me. Oh God— such mercy! I pulled over under a tree and wept. What would our family be without him? From beneath that tree I saw such justice; my dream, my error, my leg. Everything had been incredibly lucky, even to the doctor's bewilderment at my survival. Such heroes the French and Polynesian peoples had been for us. I just felt so completely grateful to everybody. And then, then—there was the Love. My family's strength its lighthouse, unspoken in the prayers that did not go unanswered, and always there somewhere in my luck—my incredible luck. Yeah, that moment under the tree really cleaned me up.

I felt myself returning—my happy self. And yet, I knew I was not really the same person. I caught myself time and again watching my fam-ily around me as if I were not there, as if I were a ghost. This was odd and a bit disturbing, but not entirely. I was thinking from a new place, and I knew I had to get used to that.

During a prolonged period of dying, the old barrier between the con-scious mind and the subconscious somehow dissolves. Likewise, invol-untary systems like the beating of your heart become voluntary; you understand that it's important to mind that your heart beats, and that your lungs breathe, but it is a decision. The fear of death evaporates. Your ego—your personal identity—evaporates.

Jean still thinks I was unconscious at times. Not so. But there has never been a way to convey to her in words where I was. I knew I needed to stay firmly in a particular state of mind, which was one of absolute awareness. Not speaking, keeping my eyes shut occasionally, were things I knew I was supposed to do at certain times—something guided me along this perilous path between awareness and conservation. I left this state briefly to speak with copilot Yves, and to speak with the medics in the air, and to tell the nurse in the ambulance in Papeete not to take my whole leg. Except for these necessary trips to the surface, I preferred to stay in the other, somehow sacred place.

I can still see the silhouettes of the surgeons above me in the operating room, with the white light above them. I cared not where I was going from there. I knew my family was safe. I was in ecstasy, not delirium. I went through a door and I came out on the other side, quite changed. When I got through my depression back home, I found myself with this new orientation to life.

So I found myself walking on the California shore with a new leg and a decent gait, and with Jean at my side and my kids playing nearby. Jack was pulling some tentacled thing up from a black reef, to the horror and amusement of the other families walking there. He told them all about whatever the thing was, and then he put it back into the sea. Our other kids were standing there in the sun and wind. Jean, as I say, was there with me. We moved down the beach like dolphins in the sea.

And we had done this thing; we had done it together.

We have a great zoo in our town. Jack has the keys, of course. We were there a few Sundays ago. I was watching a particular young couple take their kids around, introducing them to the extraordinary beauty of life on this planet. I was thinking, you know, it was nice that our family had the resources to do what we did. We worked hard to make it happen. Worked a lifetime, really. But why should anyone have to work so hard to see and feel and live the beauty of life? It's all around us. I so admired that young couple. It's all around us.

———

Now, for most folks one pair of legs lasts a lifetime, and that must be because they use them mercifully, as a tender-hearted old lady uses her roly-poly old coach-horses. But Ahab; oh he's a hard driver. Look, driven one leg to death, and spavined the other for life, and now wears out bone legs by the cord. Halloa, there, you Smut! bear a hand there with those screws, and let's finish it...

—*Herman Melville,* MOBY DICK

AFTERWORD

Jean Silverwood

I thought coming home would be the end of the horrors. Instead, John underwent a second surgery to amputate above his knee, and a third to treat a near-fatal infection; we visited him every day for three weeks in the hospital and watched him sometimes shake with convulsions.

Back at home, nurses came and went. I learned to hook up IV bottles and to clean John's leg wound pump. Dealing with the health insurance carrier was the worst of it, however. Because Tahiti's only hospital is not on our "preferred provider" list, only a small portion of the bill was covered. The prosthetic leg coverage was limited to $2000. This might have covered a peg for Captain Ahab, but a modern prosthesis costs as much as a luxury car. There would be no money from our life insurance or Social Security disability, and we didn't have regular disability insurance. Happily, our boat was covered by a London insurance company, which immediately paid in full.

Phantom pains kept John on powerful painkillers for several months. This worried me, so John switched to a non-addicting pain reliever as soon as his pain eased. He has held his spirits up most of the time and is still a loving father and husband. He swims and works out several times a week. Every Tuesday night he meets his old buddies at the AA meeting in San Diego.

Family and friends delivered meals, they babysat, they listened. This was a big help, as I was often not quite myself. Example: I bought our Christmas tree, had it tied to the roof of the car, and, without thinking, drove through an automatic car wash! I also experienced a panic attack while driving on the freeway with all the kids. I can now drive short distances, but I still don't feel comfortable on the freeways. It is a mystery how a boating accident can affect freeway driving. For me, it did.

I miss our long walks together. I am now the one to climb ladders to change bulbs, run downstairs to check on a kid, but all that doesn't count against the miracle of still having John with me. And John is constantly learning new ways to do the old things. He will be back on a bike and skis before long, I'm sure.

We used to argue for days, now it is for minutes; I have learned to let things go.

The kids are much closer now. They learned that they live extremely privileged lives compared to most of the world. I know this will move them always to help others.

Ben is now a very confident young man. He just finished his freshman year studying aerospace engineering, and he loves it. Leaving him at college was difficult for me—seeing that he is truly grown. The time we spent together will be a treasure always for me. Jack says Ben is nicer now. Camille misses him terribly, but she seems very proud of him.

Amelia is an artistic high school junior. Her passion for dance continues. She practices three hours a day, five days a week. The clothing she made on the boat has inspired her to choose a college where she can major in fashion design, or perhaps have a dual major in dance and fashion design. And she still loves to bake—any excuse to make cookies, a birthday cake, or cupcakes. The ingredients and mixing bowls are all over the kitchen, which still looks so luxuriously big.

Jack is growing up fast but is very inquisitive and tries to negotiate everything. He often tells me how he misses living on the boat, fishing every day, and seeing different places. Like the other kids, he now has a taste for many kinds of foods.

Camille has also grown, but is, as ever, a joyful child. "I miss the flying fish on deck in the morning," she told me. How wonderful to miss such a simple and beautiful thing! She went to a surf camp for a week, and her instructor said she was the best seven-year-old surfer they had ever seen. Indeed, she hops and jumps along the board as she rides in on the wave—a child of the sea.

When my father came to California for a visit, he seemed a little confused. The following month he was diagnosed with brain cancer, which soon took his life. My moment on the bow of the boat with God prepared me for his death.

Then, on an October evening, the sky darkened with smoke from distant brush fires. I closed the windows and went to bed, but the wind made sleeping difficult. I stepped outside and saw an orange glow to the east. The fire department was soon evacuating our area. The great California wildfires of 2007 were headed our way.

Amelia was awake, listening to the news and packing photos in a suitcase. She was very upset, almost frantic, "Mom you don't have time to make coffee! We need to get out of here!" She was reliving the accident and the one thing she treasured above all else were our lives and our family photos. John, Jack, and Camille were soon ready to go. We put the cat and dog in the car and left our home, not knowing if we would ever see it again. The sky was bright with flames and sparks.

After three days on the run, I carefully drove past the barricades. Our neighborhood looked like a war zone with trees and branches scattered everywhere. Helicopters were still dumping water over nearby homes. In the end, we were lucky. The fires skipped here and there toward the sea, and our home survived.

Even when I didn't know what I would see when I made the last turn up our street, I knew I had changed in those long hours holding John on a distant reef. Some things matter and some don't. You can build a new house if you must.

My gratitude for life, my continuing meditation, yoga, and volunteering has given me a sense of peace that I have never experienced before. I still have emotionally hard moments, but that just goes with having four kids and a guy like John.

I miss that special time with my children and the big smile on John's face as he took it all in. I miss the special people from different cultures whom we met. Yes, yes, I would live on a boat again. As a matter of fact, I suggested the idea to John not long ago. A place with fewer reefs, perhaps.

John Silverwood

I can get around, and pretty well, thanks to recent improvements in prosthetic limbs. Most of the improvements came about for our disabled troops, so the technology I am enjoying came with a heavy price, which I honor.

I was at first ashamed to be seen hopping along on my new leg, or without it on crutches. Jack saw me putting on the leg one morning and he said, "That thing is so cool!" He and Camille insisted I wear shorts and hobble down the driveway with them so they could show my leg off to their friends. I was soon talked into camping with Camille's YMCA Indian Princesses group on the beach. A crowd of little girls surrounded us, mesmerized by my new leg. Their questions came at me from everywhere, breathless and all at once.

"Where did you *real* leg go?"

I grinned. What else could I do? "Hey girls, you see right here? That's where it got chopped off. Right here is where my real leg starts." One of them managed to take her hands off the leg long enough to ask, "Oohh! Did it hurt? Did you cry?"

I later camped with Jack's Cub Scouts, and took my place on the bench of his Little League team, and then his football team.

Beyond these things, I needed to get on a boat, if only to show the sea and myself that I was not afraid and not defeated.

After a long flight to Auckland, New Zealand, the Van Zwams welcomed me back aboard *Fruity Fruits* for an ocean passage north to New Caledonia.

What friends are these who would take on such a wobbly sailor? We were five days at sea in unsettled winter weather, cold and wet. We rolled beneath a collision of winds rotating high above. Towering clouds and fog resembled gray cathedral walls blocking our path ahead. We spoke in muted tones, wondering how to punch through the dark wall in search of favorable winds.

Steffan nodded and said, "I don't know either," and in we went. It wasn't so bad.

ACKNOWLEDGMENTS

This section is very important to us. We have thanked many below, yet realize there are more people who have helped and guided us through this ordeal with their thoughts and prayers. Though you may not be mentioned here, please know you are remembered in our hearts. There are so many people who helped us fulfill our dream, keep us alive, and recover to face the world again we want to thank. There were so many acts of kindness and love that will not be forgotten. We would like to thank both our families for their love and support along our journey, and in helping us to heal later. The Silverwoods; Mark for coming to Tahiti to help and Rozanne for buying all the supplies needed, Pat and John, Jim and Lisa, and Ken and Wendy; and Aileen and Toby Rosvold, Jim and Joanne Boera, Albert and Claudia Boera, Carol Driscoll, Jane and Billy Foster, Kay O'Donnell, Marie and Tom McCormack, all the nieces, nephews, cousins, aunts, and uncles—and of course, to our four children, Ben, Amelia, Jack, and Camille.

To our rescuers, without whom this story would not have been told:

the Taputu family, the crew of the French Army Puma helicopter, Captain Sebastien Roger, co-captain Yves Peltrault, Doctor Bruno Volpeliere, Philippe Vanderkerckhove, Jean François Perdereau, Khaled Bentabet, Maitre Gilles Renaud. The crew of the French Navy Gardian jet, the first in the air: Captain Eric Mahoudo, Olivier Eynard, Vincent Desmidet, Daniel Raingeval, Laurent Ferry, Mechel Blanchard. And to all of MRCC Papeete's ground crew and Mahina Coastal Radio. We especially extend our deep appreciation to French Vice Admiral Patrick Giaume and his staff for the exquisite awards ceremony and luncheon held to honor the efforts of all mentioned above and for us, and to the U.S. Coast Guard, Alameda California, and especially Lt. Kevin Denicker and Ernie Delli Gatti. Thank you to Christopher Kozely, U.S. consular agent, Tahiti. Chris coordinated so many things far beyond the call of duty. To the Meridian Hotel for providing my family a wonderful place to stay while John recovered. To Marc Henrion and all our fellow cruisers who provided clothing for us. To Emily and Alan for all their transportation help, and to Laurent and Fred Hermalin for their help in taking care of *Emerald Jane.*

To the entire staff at Centre Hospitalier de la Polynesie Francaise in Papeete, Tahiti, we say: *Mauruuru!* and *Merci!,* especially to Dr. Didier Raou, Dr. Didier Hatala, Dr. Claire Frederic, and Dr. Frederic Evanat for pulling me back to life. To Serge Tapare and Bruno Vota in administration for helping get calls coming and going from the U.S. and working with AXA International Medical Assistance in arranging medical transport for John, and for carrying the frustrations of dealing with our health insurance carrier, Pacific Care. To Janet Kobilarova of AXA Insurance who was hired by our Citibank Credit card for her kindness while arranging for us to get back home. To Maureen Bethany, R.N., also of AXA for caring for John while accompanying him back to the U.S. To the staff of Scripps Memorial Hospital in La Jolla, California, especially Dr. David Hackley, for his conviction and vigilance both before and after successfully amputating my leg above the knee. To my nurse Liz, and Dr. Chang, in isolating my infection. To Kevin Calvo of Bionics, Inc., and his staff for their skill and persistence in fitting me with my prosthetic leg, and Bert Acosta of Amputees America.

Thank you to everyone at Random House, Susan Mercandetti for her insight, patience, and perserverance, Abby Plesser, Gina Centrello, Jonathan Jao, Tom Perry, Sally Marvin, Carol Schneider, Karen Fink, Megan Fishmann, Dennis Ambrose, and Beck Stvan. To Mel Berger, Mary Martin, and Laurie Pozmontier of the William Morris Agency for getting this book off the ground. To Malcolm McConnell for helping us start the story and especially to Dennis Burke for taking that story and making the book the best it could be. To my best man, Roy Trakin, an accomplished writer and true friend, for his advice during the initial planning of this story. To Larry Himmel, newscaster and friend, for putting our story on CBS affiliate KFMB. To John Riise of *Latitude 38,* John Wilkins of *The San Diego Union-Tribune,* Ken Miller of *Readers' Digest,* and to Carol Sherman for her kind advice. To doctors Ken Binmoeller, Barry Reeve, and Brigette and Xavier Frapaise, for their invaluable help in translating John's medical records.

To the Boy Scouts of America and the leaders of San Diego Troops 766 and 689 for teaching Ben the lifesaving skills that kept me alive, Jeff Jensen, Glen Doshay, Chuck Scott, Jim Depolo, Dan Claxton, John McCutchen. To the board of the Desert Pacific Counsel, especially Bob Bolingbroke, Terry Trout, and Mike Sherman for awarding Ben the Honor Medal with Crossed Palms and for teaching our young men a code of respect toward both themselves and the natural splendor of our country. To the Indian Princesses and their dads of the Coyote Nation for getting John up and running and living again so soon after the accident with their help at the beach campout. Especially to Brett Jorgensen for my first speaking engagement. To my fellow misfits at the La Jolla Men's meeting, who took me back. And to Urban Miyares and the Challenged America group for getting John out on his first sail and for all the inspiring things they do to help disabled sailors of all ages.

To the special cruisers and friends whom we've met along the way, always teaching us much and giving us the will to continue. The Van Zwam family of *Fruity Fruits,* Andrew and Michele of *Capriccio,* Andreas and Migdaly of *Cosa Nostra,* and Suni and Charlie of *Cosmos.* To Penn and Pam Coffey for their excellent help as crew for a few legs of the trip. Derek Duffield for showing us the "ropes." To Panama Canal pilot Nilo Miranda for his hospitality in Panama. And to Jim Laflin, who talked us into buying *Emerald Jane,* and Tony Chinery for selling her to us. To Father Purcell for his prayers and hospital visits, and to our friend Father Bourgeois, who led his congregation in prayers for us even as we struggled on the reef. Thank you to all our neighbors and friends who sent gifts, e-mails, letters, and cards. To the parents and friends of the Church of Nativity and Solana Santa Fe Elementary School, who delivered meals to our house and kept our kids very well fed while John was in the hospital. Thanks to all of our dear friends who helped in many different ways, Leslie Boren for flying to Tahiti and Ron for helping here, Leslie and Teddy Aroney, Maxine and Gary Kreitzer, Jeanne and Paul Stryker, Joan Himmel, Susan and Eric Fuller, Jill Trakin, Sydney and Don Vale, Ann and Bob Lena, Lynne and Andrew Young, Diane and David Bell, Barbara and Bay Ponder, Kerry and Julie Garza, Kathe and Larry Reischman, Bill Chipman, Deandrea and Jeff Brazel, Stephanie and Bob Teshima, and Yanina and Mark Adler.

ABOUT THE AUTHORS

JOHN and JEAN SILVERWOOD live with their family
in San Diego County, California.